CALIFORNIA GOVERNMENT AND POLITICS ANNUAL 1993-94

EDITED BY THOMAS R. HOEBER & CHARLES M. PRICE

CALIFORNIA
JOURNAL
PRESS

Copyright© 1993 by Information for Public Affairs, Inc.
Published by California Journal Press, 1714 Capitol
Avenue, Sacramento, CA 95814.
ISBN: 0-930302-90-7
ISSN: 0084-8271

INTRODUCTION

The California Phenomenon

The California system of government is the same in bold outline as the government of the United States, with three theoretically equal branches of government operating under the supreme law of the land, the Constitution. Nevertheless, there are some significant differences:

• The California Constitution is far more detailed than the United States Constitution and, thus, the Governor and the Legislature have far less power and freedom than the President and Congress. Matters that are left to the statute-writers in Washington are covered in detail in the California Constitution, taking these issues out of the hands of the Governor and Legislature. The judiciary, on the other hand, may be even more powerful because this branch is in charge of interpreting the constitution.

• Normally, the speaker of the Assembly has far more power in Sacramento than any single member of Congress in Washington because this official controls virtually all committee appointments. Few bills pass over the speaker's objection. However the power of particular speakers ebbs and flows depending on factors such as their personalities, the size of their party's majority and the loyalty of their parties caucus.

• The people at large have much more control over California government than over national government because they have the powers of initiative, referendum and recall, giving them the ultimate voice in all matters that are not in conflict with the United States Constitution. Most major fiscal decisions, such as the enactment of general-obligation bond issues and the raising of local taxes, also cannot be made without voter approval.

Other factors make California unique as well. It has been the land of superb climate, breathtaking natural scenery, rapid growth, and the glamor of movie stars and the radio and television industries. Its government and politics reflect the excitement of a land of opportunity and colorful characters, and the news media look to California for the bizarre and offbeat. These unique characteristics may be fading, however. No longer is California the promised land; smog has dulled the horizon; unemployment runs higher than elsewhere; and the movie industry is far from what it used to be. California is experiencing the ills of a mature society: slowed financial growth, reduced national defense spending with the end of the Cold War, declining infrastructure, burgeoning population, especially among new immigrants from foreign lands, and the need for urban renewal. The Los Angeles race riot of 1992 (the worst ever in the nation), sparked by the beating of African-American Rodney King by four white police officers and their acquittal by a Simi Valley jury, is indicative of California's urban malaise. California, in short, is no longer the land of milk and honey.

Constitution

Every few years the California Legislature prints a paperback book with up-to-date versions of the United States and California Constitutions. The document that is the basic law of the entire nation takes up 27 pages; but the California Constitution takes up three times as much space (and twice as much just for the index).

The state constitution contains 21 articles describing, in great detail the bill of rights, the powers of various branches of government and basic state law in such fields as education, local government, corporations, taxation, water, harbor frontages, state debt, homesteading, motor vehicles, civil service, open space, public housing, and even the minimum drinking age.

The California Constitution wasn't always such a long-winded document. The first constitution, adopted in 1849 (one year before California was admitted into the Union), was a basic statement of the rights of the people and the responsibility of the three branches of government. Peter H.

Burnett was elected California's first governor in November 1849, and the first Legislature convened shortly thereafter to levy taxes, establish cities and counties, put the courts into operation, and borrow enough money to grease the wheels of state government. Over the next 30 years, only three major changes were made to this constitution. This stands in sharp contrast to the current practice of adopting amendments every election year.

Massive unrest produced a greatly expanded new constitution in 1879. There was tremendous distrust of the state government, especially the Legislature, and demands were made for greater public control over taxation. The state's population had increased 17-fold in its first three decades. A drought and unfavorable economic conditions had produced mass unemployment. The railroad bloc practically ran the state and was an obvious target. Farmers were in revolt against the railroads and other businessmen. Unemployed whites joined the Workingman's Party to seek a ban against imported Chinese labor. Constitutional reform was seen as a solution, and a convention was called in 1878. The result was an extremely detailed document, which was adopted the next year by a comfortable but not overwhelming margin. The document remains the basic law of California, although it has been amended hundreds of times.

But despite the goals of those who demanded the convention, the second constitution did not provide major reform. That was to come later with Hiram Johnson and the Progressives, who instituted the initiative, referendum and recall.

Amending the Constitution

There are three ways amendments to the California Constitution may be placed on the ballot for approval by a majority of the voters: by initiative petition now requiring over 600,000 signatures of registered voters, by legislative proposal, and by constitutional convention.

• *The initiative.* Almost every election California voters decide the fate of one or more measures placed on the ballot through the initiative process. The initiative was designed as a method of exerting public control over the Legislature, so that bills ignored by the lawmakers could be put into effect. In recent years, elected officials themselves have sponsored initiatives when they are unable to get their way in the Legislature. Beginning in the late 1970's the initiative has been used more and more frequently by special interest groups, the very element the initiative was created to counter. The initiative can also be used to enact statutes.

• *Legislative proposal.* Every year, legislators introduce dozens of proposed constitutional amendments. A small percentage receive the necessary two-thirds vote of each house to qualify for the ballot. A 1983 law requires that ballot measures be numbered consecutively from election to election, starting with November 1982, to avoid confusion. Thus, for example, the November 1990 ballot measures were numbered 124 to 151.

• *Convention.* The constitution provides that the Legislature may call a constitutional convention by a two-thirds vote of both houses. However, it has not done so since 1878. Instead the Legislature has chosen to form a revision commission because it can control the commission and its recommendations. Such a commission existed from 1963 to 1970. The commission had some successes during those years and managed to reduce the size of the constitution considerably. From time to time sentiment is expressed for re-establishing the commission to continue the work of streamlining the state's supreme legal document. 🏛

Reprinted from *California Journal*, January 1992

California had scarcely two million citizens in 1909 when Lord James Bryce, British ambassador to the United States, visited the state and asked a prophetic question: "What will happen when California is filled by 50 millions of people and its valuation is five times what it is now? There will be more people — as many as the country can support — and the real question will be not about making more wealth or having more people, but whether the people will then be happier

Dan Walters is a political columnist for The Sacramento Bee *and author of "The New California." This article is a shortened version of Chapter 1 of the second edition of "The New California," due for publication in February.*

or better than they have been hitherto or are at this moment."

Eighty-plus years later, California is more than halfway toward that 50-million mark and has become America's most diverse, most populous and most economically, culturally and politically potent state. But without knowing it, Californians are still seeking answers to Lord Bryce's question as they career toward the 21st Century.

From San Ysidro to Susanville, from Ventura to Volcano, from Moreno Valley to Moraga, no region of the state is being left untouched as California fashions a 21st Century civilization like nothing ever seen on the North American continent: ethnically complex, with distinct socio-economic classes; competitive; technologically sophisticated; older and more harried; and, unless a cadre of new civic and political leader-

ship emerges, a society that loses its communal identity and evolves into a collection of mutually hostile tribes.

California's once-powerful industrial economy, created during the emergency of World War II and later expanded to serve both Cold War and civilian demands, has given way to a post-industrial hybrid economy that rests on multiple bases and resembles that of a major nation more than that of a typical American state.

In a single generation, hundreds of lumber mills, auto and tire factories, steel plants, canneries, railroad yards, shipyards and other basic industries have closed. Of those that survive, many have downgraded their wage structures to meet foreign competition. Deregulation of trucking, telephone service and airlines has made them more competitive but also has forced

Ethnicity

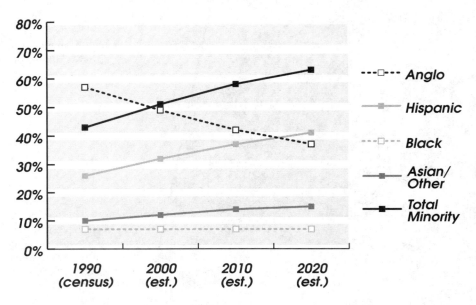

their employees to accept lower wages. And the new industrial jobs that have been created, especially those in high-tech and services, are overwhelmingly non-union, with non-professional wage scales in the sub-$12 per hour range.

At the same time, whole new industries have emerged, based on trade with burgeoning Pacific Rim nations, on highly sophisticated technology and on information; new industries that created three million jobs during the 1980s and allowed California to absorb a record increase in population while lowering its unemployment rate before a severe recession took told in 1990.

Between traditional industry's contraction and new industry's expansion lie the seeds of socio-economic stratification. Opportunities for the children of the postwar industrial middle class have been reduced, or at least become more contrasting. They and the young immigrants who continue to pour into California must either prepare themselves for expanding opportunities in technical, managerial, creative and professional fields or be content with relatively low-paying service industry jobs.

California's work force, therefore, is being squeezed like a tube of toothpaste: an expanding overclass at the top, earning the $40,000-plus salaries, buying the homes, living the California

good life; and an exploding underclass at the bottom, ill-educated, ill-served by overburdened social services, struggling to find affordable housing, forgoing medical care and seeing the doors of opportunity become more difficult to open; and an economic and social middle that stagnates or even declines. And it is a change that is punctuated by the state's rapidly evolving ethnic structure, one in which today's minorities will soon become the collective majority. The economic and social differences are likely to become more distinct as California continues to move away from the egalitarian ideal.

Economists Leon Bouvier and Philip Martin, in a mid-1980s peek into California's future for the Washington-based Population Reference Bureau, described that scenario as "the possible emerging of a two-tier economy with Asians and non-Hispanic whites competing for high-status positions while Hispanics and Blacks struggle to get the low-paying service jobs." They noted that since 1970, "employment growth has shifted from high-wage manufacturing and government sectors to the lower-wage trade and service firms that are most likely to hire unskilled immigrants..."

End-of-decade economic data verified their prediction. Between 1982 and 1990, California's manufacturers added about a quarter-million jobs, but the service

and trade sectors created nearly two million. Between 1972 and 1989, manufacturing dropped from nearly 21 percent of the state's jobs to about 17 percent. Jobs at the lower end of the scale ($5000 to $15,000 per year) and those at the upper end ($40,000 to $50,000 per year) grew two to three times faster than middle-income jobs ($25,000 to $30,000 per year). Increasingly, California families have achieved or clung to middle-class status only by merging paychecks of two or more workers.

There are strong indications that these trends will continue in the 1990s. The state Employment Development Department estimates that total California employment will increase by nearly one-third between 1987 and 2000, from 11.7 million to 15.4 million jobs, with above-average increases in trade, finance and services, and sub-par growth in manufacturing, transportation, communication, mining and government categories. The Center for the Continuing Study of the California Economy is even more optimistic, seeing employment in the state approach 17.5 million by 2000 with job and personal-income growth rates in the 1990s that are far above those of the nation as a whole and outstripping even population growth.

"This is probably California's last great growth surge," said economist Stephen Levy of the Palo Alto-based economic study center. "It is entirely possible that the state's population, which will go from 30 million to 40 million in 20 years, may never each the 50-million mark." Levy said that lower birth rates should slow California's population growth after 2010.

There is, however, dissent from some economists who believe that California peaked out in the 1980s and now faces a bleak economic future because of its deteriorating infrastructure and a competitive posture vis-a-vis other states and nations. They have noted a seemingly accelerated abandonment of California by major employers, especially manufacturers, who shift or expand plants in other states and nations because of California's above-average operational costs.

George Salem, a banking analyst for Prudential Securities, created a stir in California economic circles in 1991 when he circulated a report suggesting that the state "shows new evidence of structural weakness" and could face the kind of severe economic dislocation that struck Massachusetts and Texas during the 1980s.

At the time that Salem delivered his startling verdict, the state was experiencing a severe recession, with unemployment having jumped more than 2 percent since the go-go days of the 1980s. During the first year of the recession, from mid-1990 to mid-1991, the state lost an astonishing 380,000 jobs — roughly a year's employment growth during the expansive years of the 1980s. And despite the recession, which economists said was exacerbated by such localized factors as a record freeze and cutbacks in military procurement spending, California continued to experience huge levels of migration and child birth that drove its population upward by some 800,000 persons a year, thus raising doubts whether the state could continue to absorb newcomers or would face a future of continued economic uncertainty.

At the very least, the recession accelerated the evolution from an industrial to a post-industrial economy and thus the stratification of California society.

And if stratification happens, it may set the stage for a 21st Century political climate that pits haves against have-nots, with the political middle declining along with the economic middle and both major parties being compelled to realign themselves to the new socio-economic reality. Lewis Butler and Bruce Kelley of California Tomorrow, an organization devoted to worrying about California's future, use a harsh term to describe what is happening: segregation. This can be avoided, they wrote in 1989, only if people of different classes, colors and cultures live, work and go to school together.

The data of change, gleaned from a variety of public and private sources, is staggering:

• California's population, less than 16 million in 1960, grew by nearly 50 percent to 23.8 million by 1980, hit 30 million by 1990 and is expected to top 36 million by 2000 and climb to more than 40 million by 2010.

• The Anglo population (what demographers call "non-Hispanic white") is virtually stagnant. In fact, the Anglo population may begin to decline before the turn of the century, and a low Anglo birthrate means that its portion of the population is growing older faster than others, with median age already at least 15 years higher than the non-Anglo population.

• Some three-quarters of the near-term population growth and nearly all long-term growth is among Hispanics and Asians. California already is home to more than a third of the Asians who live in the United States, and the proportion of Californians who have Asian ancestry swelled from 4 percent to 10 percent in just a decade, replacing blacks as the state's third-largest major ethnic group.

• The Hispanic population, meanwhile, is being expanded by a high level of legal and illegal immigration from Latin America, mostly Mexico, and by a birthrate that is nearly twice that of Anglos. Demographers expect the continued political unrest and economic chaos in Latin America to push millions of Latino immigrants across a porous border into California, and even economic reform in Mexico will not have a major impact on that trend for years.

• The Black population is relatively stagnant, fixed at under 8 percent of the total; it's not shrinking but grows only at the rate of the overall population.

• Sometime before 2000, perhaps as early as 1996, Anglos will be a minority for the first time — a decade earlier than demographers had expected in the mid-1980s. A generation later, Hispanics and Anglos will be about equal in population, approximately 38 percent each.

• Despite an evening-out of population among the state's large ethnic groups, there are growing disparties in education and economic attainment. Hispanics and Blacks are far more likely to drop out of high school and less likely to obtain college educations than either Anglos or Asians, thereby becoming less able to compete for the well-paying professional and technical jobs that California is continuing to produce.

• With high birthrates among recent immigrants, the overall status of California's children has deteriorated markedly in recent years. A quarter of California's mothers are unwed and disproportionately high numbers of newborn babies suffer from low birth weights, drug addictions and other maladies. And as vaccination rates for children decline, once-conquered childhood diseases such as measles are staging alarming comebacks.

• Some 20 percent of California's 30 million residents lack any kind of health insurance, either private or public. This accounts for 20 percent of the nation's uninsured, even though the state contains just over 12 percent of the American population.

But the signs of change are to be found in more than numbers. They are to be found in the changing California landscape. They are found in such places as Moreno Valley, a small community in the semi-desert of Riverside County, which was the state's fastest-growing county in the 1980s. Moreno Valley just became a city in the mid-1980s and within a few months had a population of more than 100,000, mostly young families. It was graphic evidence of one of the most important social trends of the 1980s: dispersal of the economy and population from coastal enclaves to interior valleys and hills.

That phenomenon was fueled, in part, by the changes in the economy, especially the advent of portable jobs in burgeoning technical and service fields — jobs that do not depend on proximity to raw materials or even to transportation centers and that can be moved out of traditional urban employment centers and into the suburbs, thus allowing workers to move even further into the countryside for more pleasant surroundings and less-expensive housing. The move to the interior is evident from Escondido in northern San Diego through San Bernardino and Riverside counties to the Central Valley as far north as Redding.

It is largely, however, a movement of Anglos. And it contributes, as do continued high rates of immigration, to radical social surgery on the face of California's cities. As whites flee the cities, their places are taken by foreign immigrants who pack themselves ever more densely into stocks of housing that are not expanding.

Los Angeles, the new American melting pot, lost 500,000 Anglos between 1970 and 1980 and is headed for a 60 percent Hispanic population by the turn of the century. There are more than 100 separate languages spoken at Los Angeles area schools, 75 of them at Hollywood High School alone. Conversely, San Francisco, once a polyglot, is becoming a Beverly Hills-like enclave of the Anglo-Asian affluent, driving its middle classes to the suburbs and its Blacks across the bay to Oakland by development policies that favor high-income professionals. One-time farm towns of the Central Valley are diversifying their economies and flirting with metropolitan status.

In addition, whole regions of the

state, especially those north of the San Francisco-Sacramento axis, have seen their basic industries of timber and agriculture decline and nothing emerge to replace them. The result: economic and social stagnation that forces the young to seek jobs in growth areas.

The growth in and changing composition of California's population during the next 30 to 40 years will put an incredible strain on transportation systems, water supplies, sewage treatment, housing supply, educational facilities — what those in the public policy trade call "infrastructure." The California Economic Development Corporation has warned that without a massive overhaul of transportation policies, traffic congestion will increase by 15 percent a year.

Local officials throughout the state, especially in high-growth areas, already feel the strain and are compelled to take extraordinary steps to deal with it. But as they and state officials seek the billions of dollars needed to build and staff public facilities, they collide with another phenomenon that evolved in 1980s California: resistance to new taxes among voters who are not representative of the diverse new California but carry-overs from an earlier era. At the precise moment that California's political leaders confront a society that grows more complex as it grows numerically, California's voters are numerically stagnant, overwhelmingly white, middle-aged and middle-class, with conservative atttitudes toward taxes first felt with the passage of Proposition 13 in 1978 but still being expressed in the 1990s. The effect of these twin, contradictory pressures is to contribute to the political confusion and deadlock that marked the 1980s.

Politicians fear voter backlash if they propose new government programs, or expand old programs due to the pressures from expanded caseloads. And both the state and local governments have direct restraints on spending imposed by a Proposition 13 aftermath (Proposition 4), approved by voters in 1979 and modified only slightly in 1990.

The Legislature, moreover, has become preoccupied with internal power struggles and a series of image-bending scandals. Both it and the governor of the 1980s, Republican George Deukmejian, seemed disinterested in dealing with the far-reaching public policy issues that dynamic socio-economic change creates. Instead, they

played games of political one-upsmanship that led to an explosion of initiative ballot measures that also contributed to the state's political paralysis. As the 1990s dawned, many were openly saying that California may have become ungovernable in traditional terms.

That was what Stu Spencer, a veteran Republican political strategist, told U.S. Senator Pete Wilson when Wilson, fresh off a Senate re-election victory in 1988, began thinking about running for governor in 1990. But Wilson, pressured by state and national Republican leaders to run and keep the Capitol in GOP hands for the all-critical reapportionment that was to follow the 1990 census, decided to run anyway. Wilson defeated Democrat Dianne Feinstein, the former mayor of San Francisco, in the November 1990 election. But the fact that both candidates came from the political middle indicated that voters yearned for new leadership.

Wilson came into office in 1991 determined to make California's government work again by shifting emphasis from remedial to preventive in education and social services and by proposing a first-ever statewide growth-management program aimed at bringing some order to the state's chaotic development patterns. But Wilson faced a monstrous state budget crisis born of recession and of a decade of ignoring the conflict between anti-tax fever and huge levels of population growth. He faced, too, a Legislature that was beset by scandal and torn apart by factional and partisan infighting.

As the traditional forms of governance lock up, what may be emerging is a new form of quasi-public, quasi-private governance in which local economic and civic interests, working in concert with local governments, create new vehicles for the improvement of infrastructure. In Santa Clara County, for example, the high-tech industry supported a successful drive to persuade local voters to raise sales taxes to finance better highways after it became apparent that more aid would not be forthcoming from Sacramento. Dozens of other counties followed suit and, in a rare major policy action in the Capitol, Deukmejian and legislators agreed on a comprehensive transportation-financing plan eventually enacted by voters in 1990.

Bond issues, lease-purchase contracts and other forms of creative financing have been used by local officials to finance infrastructure improvements.

But as with other aspects of California culture, it is widening the gap between the haves and the have-nots and weakening the bonds of a broader community. Affluent, growing areas can afford to make such improvements while poor areas with stagnant economies cannot. In 21st Century California, what kind of highways serve motorists, how crowded the schools, how dependable the water supply may depend on where one lives.

The demands of affluent parents for better elementary and high school education got results in Sacramento. But California has continued to lag behind in its overall educational performance, especially in services to the non-affluent, non-Anglo and non-English speakers, as it struggled to cope with record growth in school enrollment. By 1990, the average Latino adult in California had three fewer years of education than Anglo, Asian or Black adults.

Dropout rates among minorities showed little improvement in the 1980s. The community college system, once California's traditional educational ladder for the economically disadvantaged, drifted in the 1980s, a victim of post-Proposition 13 budget restraints and a seeming lack of purpose. Finally, in the late 1980s, there was an effort to revive the system and redirect it back to its original purpose, but no one was certain the reforms would work.

Although California's minority population is growing faster than the Anglo population, the state's public and private universities and colleges remain bastions of Anglo and Asian aspirations. Hispanics, now more than 25 percent of the population, represented less than 10 percent of the undergraduate enrollment at the University of California in 1988, while Blacks were less than 5 percent. Asians were nearly 30 percent of UC's undergraduate enrollment — three times their proportion of the overall population.

California's public schools, anticipating the change that will occur in the larger population a decade years later, acquired a non-Anglo student population in the late 1980s even as they absorbed growth rates that approached 200,000 a year.

But the public school system is producing widely disparate results.

According to the California Postsecondary Education System, only 3.6 percent of 1985's Black high school graduates and 4.9 percent of Hispanic high school graduates were eligible for University of California admission; 13 percent of Anglo graduates and 26 percent of Asians were qualified. Asians, even those who only recently migrated from Southeast Asia, are doing very well in the state's schools — a by-product, sociologists believe, of the Asian cultural impetus to excel that may be missing from other minorities.

The high level of Asian education and economic achievement, markedly above those of the population as a whole, has led many demographers to see them as part of an Anglo-Asian overclass that will dominate California's two-tier society of the 21st Century.

And if the elementary and high schools become dominated by Hispanic and Black students while an aging and stagnant Anglo population produces relatively few school-age children — and sends many of them to private schools — it is questionable whether the overclass will be willing to invest the money in public education. One poll taken for the California Teachers Association indicates that older, white voters are less supportive of public education that other groups; by one estimate, fewer than 20 percent of California voters are parents of public school students and the percentage is declining.

Some Hispanic and Black leaders fear that public education, and especially programs geared to the needs of their children, will be neglected in the 21st Century by a dominant class that has little direct interest in it. Indeed, some see Proposition 13 and its anti-government, anti-tax aftershocks as the first indications of growing disinterest.

Because of myriad pressures, California's political structure in the 1980s seemed incapable of dealing with the change. With professionalization of the Legislature and rising partisanship, the Capitol in the 1980s evolved into a place where the petty concerns of internal politics came to dominate the more pressing needs of the real world. In the largest context, political leaders could not simultaneously meet the needs of the state's large and diverse population and obey the mandates of its politically active and somewhat conservative middle and upper-middle classes.

That tension, which increased steadily during the decade, resulted in an explosion of ballot measures whose fate, both positive and negative, did little to clarify the situation.

If California is evolving into a two-tier society as present trends indicate, it will have vast political consequences. There seems to be an overall swing toward conservatism and the Republican Party in California already. As the state was voting overwhelmingly for President Ronald Reagan's re-election in 1984, for example, it also was giving a plurality of its votes to Republican congressional candidates — despite the fact that a partisan congressional redistricting plan enacted in 1982 handed firm control of the congressional delegation to Democrats.

Pollster Mervin Field reported in 1985 that his survey of voter identification shows the GOP having drawn even with the Democrats for the first time in recent history, a trend that held firm as the 1980s evolved into the 1990s. Democratic voter registration, which approached 60 percent in the mid-1970s, slipped below 50 percent for the first time in more than 50 years.

It seems that Anglo voters and middle- to upper-income Asians and Hispanics are identifying more strongly with the Republican Party. And while they may be outnumbered in the overall population, they are most likely to register and to vote.

Lower-income Hispanics and Asians are not participating in California's political process. Asians have the overall lowest levels of political activity of any ethnic group; by 1990, they were 10 percent of the state's population but scarcely 2 percent to 3 percent of the dependable voters. Blacks are more politically active — and overwhelmingly Democratic — but are a stagnant or even declining portion of the state's population. The industrial middle class, the traditional backbone of the Democratic Party, is shrinking because of economic changes.

These trends create a huge dilemma for the Democratic Party. To appeal to the overclass, it must move its ideological identity to the right, putting less stress on providing government programs to the poor. In doing so, it turns its back on some of its most active constituencies and on the liberal ideological bent of its current leaders. But to organize the unorganized runs the risk of further alienating Anglo, middle-income voters and faces enormous barriers of language, non-citizenship and a lack of political tradition among newly arrived immigrants.

The most likliey political scenario for California in the 1990s, and at least the early years of the 21st century, is for dominance by an affluent, politically active overclass using its position to protect its privileges against the larger but weaker underclass. It's a social situation that benefits the Republican Party, which has undergone a quiet evolution into a decidedly more moderate institution as it has expanded its reach. That shift is personified by Governor Wilson, a one-time party pariah for his centrist views. If the Wilsonite philosophy — tough on crime, conservative on taxes and spending; liberal on abortion and environmental issues — becomes the dominant image of the Republican Party, Democrats may be doomed to minority party status in the nation's largest state.

Evolving political power, however, is just one aspect, and probably not the most important one, of a unique culture that continually redefines itself as it expands and diversifies. Clearly, some of California's golden sheen has been tarnished by its social and economic complexities: tangled freeways, high housing prices, rising fear of crime and congested public facilities. A 1989 Field Institute poll revealed a sharp drop in Californians' sense of pride about living in the state. In previous polls, about 75 percent of those responding had rated California "one of the best places to live." But the 1989 poll saw that drop to under 60 percent.

There is some evidence that California's crushing social and economic problems are sinking in on both the state's civic leadership and the larger population. Cadres of civic leaders have been formed, both statewide and at regional and local levels, to explore workable approaches to such pithy issues as regional government, education, water, growth and, most of all, rising levels of social friction.

"California is just entering what may be its most crucial decades since the Mexican War ended in the 1840s," Bouvier and Martin conclude in their study of the state. "The state will never be the same; yet, as with the nation, it remains unfinished. ... The important question is: How will the state adjust to these demographic changes and all their repercussions?"

It's a question whose answer, if anything, is becoming more elusive. 🏛

photo by Rich Pedroncelli/photo manipulation by Patty Lyn Tweten

The longshot bid to split California

By CHARLES PRICE

Reprinted from *California Journal* August 1992

Charles Price is a professor of political science at California State University, Chico, and a frequent contributor to California Journal.

Across the globe, political change has come with dizzying speed in the past decade. Gone are the Soviet Union, Yugoslavia and Czechoslovakia, replaced by more than a dozen new nations. Closer to the United States, the province of Quebec is agitating to secede from Canada and form a new, independent nation on our northern border.

Now add to this the movement led by indefatigable Republican Assemblyman Stan Statham of Oak Run to divide California.

Why divide the state? Statham contends that citizens are intensely frustrated by the gridlock of our present government. "I am proposing a solution. It may not be a perfect solution — but it is worth trying. If you are trying to do a job that is too much for one person, doesn't it make sense to split the job? It is inevitable that we divide."

Statham's is but the latest in a long series of failed split-the-state proposals. While virtually all of the proposals generated in the last 50 years have been launched in the rural north because of southern dominance at the Capitol, earlier this century it was *Southern* California political leaders who wanted to divide the state because the government was then controlled by *Northern* interests. Other, recent divide-the-state proposals include:

• **(1941) The State of Jefferson.** This was an effort of some local officials from California's northern-most counties to secede and join with southern Oregon counties to form the new state of Jefferson. The outbreak of World War II cut short this attempt.

• **(1965) The States of Northern and Southern California.** This was state Senator Richard Dolwig's plan. His proposal called for dividing the state at the Tehachapi Mountains at the southern end of the San Joaquin Valley. Intriguingly, cities in the south, such as

Santa Barbara and Bakersfield, would have been part of Northern California under this plan.

- **(1970) The states of Eastern and Western California.** This was Democratic (formerly Republican) state Senator Randolph Collier's plan to divide California into two states: the western-urban-coastal; and the rural-interior.
- **(1974) The state of Mendocino.** This was the plan of Robin White and several northern local politicans to divide the state north of San Francisco and Sacramento with the northern portion being called Mendocino.
- **(1978) The state of Alta.** This was the proposal of Democratic state Senator Barry Keene, who, in effect, resuscitated the old Dolwig concept.
- **(1850-?) The state of Nevada.** This has been the long-shared dream of some Lassen County officials. They want their county to divorce California and marry Nevada. Indeed, Peter Lassen, namesake of the county, had formerly served as governor of Nevada. Locals contend with some justification that Reno and Carson City are much closer to Susanville in heart and geography than is Sacramento — particularly in winter months.

Given the previous failures of dividing California, few took seriously Assemblyman Statham's October 1991 call to divide the state. Some viewed the proposal as mainly a warning that rural Northern California was hurting. Indeed, several northeastern counties (Butte and Lassen in particular) face imminent bankruptcy, and most of the others are fiscal basket cases. Rural county officials have bitterly assailed state mandates imposed on them by distant Sacramento pols as the cause of their financial plight.

Others viewed the Statham proposal as a tongue-in-cheek effort to garner some favorable publicity for the veteran assemblyman. After all, for years the plaque on Statham's Assembly office door had read, "Assemblyman Stan Statham, representing the 51st state." Finally, some viewed the Statham plan as a cynical waste of time, diverting attention from California's "real" problems — budget, race, unemployment, water, health care, *ad infinitum.*

Following up on Statham's call for division, the Assembly Office of Research drafted a report to explore the feasibility of the break-up. The report noted, "The state's massive population (nearly 31 million people, followed by New York with 18 million) and geographical size which, in turn, complicate the efficient governing of California as a single unit, is the best argument for splitting the state."

There are two other advantages to division, according to the AOR. One would be to provide California, now grossly under-represented in the U.S. Senate, with two additional members. Another would be to reduce the number of people legislators represent, allowing them to be more attuned to their constituents. (Of course, the present Legislature's size could be doubled or quadrupled, or it could be made unicameral, and it would achieve the same objective of fewer people per election district — without dividing the state.)

Statham's calls for secession initially were met with a strong surge of support in northern counties. The state budget crisis, northern counties' fiscal distress, the Los Angeles riots, environmental restrictions, along with fears of ever-more millions of gallons of water being "expropriated" from Northern California and shipped southward, contributed to their receptiveness. Also, many of the same sentiments that propelled the Ross Perot presidential boom and the anti-incumbent, pro-term limits movements overlap into the divide-the-state, protest effort.

Under the federal Constitution, a state can be divided if the state legislature affected and Congress consent. The single exception to this rule, Texas, an independent nation upon its annexation to the United States, was given the subsequent right to divide into as many as five states if it so chose. Historically, Vermont was carved out of New York, Maine from Massachusetts, Kentucky from Virginia. Of course, all of these splits occurred long ago in the 18th and 19th centuries.

In order to get the state Legislature to approve a split, particularly given the fact that so many legislators represent Southern California constituencies fearful of a cut-off of northern water, Statham decided to apply ballot box pressure. Thus, county boards of supervisors were asked to place a non-binding advisory referendum on their ballots, asking voters whether they favored division. After six months of intense effort, Statham and his staff were able to persuade 31 (out of 58) counties to put the division question on the June 1992 ballot. In eight of these counties a follow-up question was added: If the state were divided, in which portion would you prefer our county to be?

Humboldt was the only far northern county that did not vote on the division question in June. Statham said, "Four of the supervisors in Humboldt County are Democrats, and they saw this as a Republican plot. In San Bernardino County [another non-participant in the referendum], supervisors saw this as a Willie Brown Democratic plot and kept it off the ballot. So, this obviously means that there are some serious DNA deficiencies on these two boards of supervisors." It is important to note that no southern and only some central California counties had the division vote on their June ballots.

To win converts to his cause, Statham hit the media circuit this past spring. He was on nearly 50 radio talk shows (mainly, but not exclusively, in this state), was interviewed on some 25 radio and television shows — including the Home Shopping Network — and his divide-the-state proposal was featured in all of the state's major newspapers and many smaller papers. The concept also has been of interest in foreign newspapers, such as Japan's *Asahi Shimbun* and the *London Times,* as well as Radio Free Europe and the BBC. Dividing the state has been discussed on Rush Limbaugh's nationally syndicated talk show and has provided monologue patter for Jay Leno on "The Tonight Show." Statham also has hired the Stoorza, Ziegaus and Metzger public-relations firm to assist in the effort.

In all, 27 of 31 counties voted in support of a state division.

While most Northern Californians strongly supported division, the 20 northern counties that gave at least 60 percent to the proposal constitute only about 4 percent of state voters. Support dwindled in southern counties.

After reviewing the 31 county voting results in June, Statham decided he had to modify his north-south split into a three-way division of Northern, Central and Southern California. Statham was convinced that Bay Area, Wine Country and San Joaquin Valley counties that had either narrowly approved or voted against separation did so mainly because they did not want to be lumped together with Southern California.

After the vote of the counties, Assembly Speaker Willie Brown an-

North California

Population	2,350,725
Budget	$3.6 billion

Number of counties:	28
Number of states in the U.S. with smaller population:	17
Number of states with smaller budget:	24

Central California

Population	10,146,200
Budget	$15 billion

Number of counties:	22
Number of states in the U.S. with smaller population:	42
Number of states with smaller budget:	47

South California

Population	17,853,900
Budget	$27 billion

Number of counties:	8
Number of states in the U.S. with smaller population:	48/49
Number of states with smaller budget:	48/49

ALTERED STATES

nounced the formation of a select committee to Divide the State to be chaired by Statham to include Republican colleague David Knowles and Democrats  Lloyd Connelly, Jack O'Connell and Dick Floyd. The select panel will draft a joint resolution to divide California into three states generally along the guidelines Statham proposed. Each of the three states would be roughly equivalent in per-capita fiscal resources.

If approved by the Legislature, the division resolution would be placed on the next statewide ballot. If a majority of voters approve, Congress (both houses) would then be  asked to give approval to the three-state division. Once this happens, constitutional commissions would be established in the three Californias to draft constitutions, determine the size of their state legislatures and whether term limits should be imposed, decide on the name of their state and select a capital site. The very earliest this could occur would be in 1995.

Statham believes that his chances of getting a favorable legislative vote will be enhanced by the fact there will be many freshman legislators elected this November. Moreover, state cutbacks in local government funding because of the budget crisis should further fuel secessionist sentiment. Additionally, Speaker Brown has for years supported dividing the state. Brown stated in a recent *Sacramento Bee* article, "It's [division] the only shot I got at governor. I know I don't have a fair shot in Orange County."

Notwithstanding these factors, it will be *very* difficult to get both houses of the Legislature to approve by majority vote the select panel's division maps. Statham's hope is that ambivalent legislators may be persuaded to vote for the resolution because it would have to be submitted to the electorate for majority approval before going to Congress. Certainly, most, but not all, of the handful of northern legislators would be supportive, but whether central and, in particular, southern legislators in sufficient numbers would vote to approve what Statham describes as a "no-fault divorce" is highly questionable.

If the proposal were approved by the Legislature and went on a statewide ballot, most citizens in rural Northern California would be supportive, though some who voted for the split previously as a way of protesting might pull back if they thought it had a chance of succeeding. Statham is convinced that many Central and Southern Californians would be supportive. "If there is any place in the United States that needs to have a new state government so that it can get special attention for all of its internal problems, it is Southern California. They need a legislature all of their own and two U.S. senators who can concentrate 101 percent of their time on gridlocked traffic, dirty air, random shootings and riots."

How Congress might react to a resolution to divide California is not clear. Mark  Powers, Statham's chief of staff, argues that Congress might be likely to dismiss the request if it came solely from the Legislature. But since it would arrive with the backing of the electorate, Congress would have to be more sympathetic.

Non-California House members might find some advantage to splitting the state because it would split the clout of the huge, 52-strong California House delegation. However, given all of the profound ideological/partisan divisions among California House members, they have seldom been a unified force anyway.

The 100 members of the U.S. Senate are members of the nation's most exclusive club. Would they be sympathetic to extending membership privileges to four add-on's? It seems highly unlikely. However, Senate Republicans might be encouraged to be supportive because they would probably gain two U.S. senators from Northern California, but Central and Southern California could counterbalance this by electing Democrats. Finally, if Congress were to agree to a California split, would this not open the door to divide-the-state movements in states like New York, Washington or Kansas?

Would Congress want to open this Pandora's box?

Finally, if California were divided into three states, would the lives of Californians be improved? Statham reassuringly argues that water would continue to flow north to south under a three-state format. "Much of the state's water is controlled by the federal government. The only difference would be that water battles would be fought inter-state rather than intra-state." But, would this reassurance allay southern fears? Statham emphasizes that the state's universities, prisons, retirement systems could all be quickly reassigned in a three-state system. "I would prefer for the UC and CSU systems to stay part of one system administered by a three-state compact. But, if the select committee panel decides to break up the system, we could make sure that no out-of-state payments would have to be made for Californians coming from any of the three parts of California." In any case, sorting out the legal nuances could keep lawyers employed for decades.

While there would be some initial start-up costs for new state office buildings and capitols in Northern and Southern California (central would already have Sacramento), Statham is convinced that this would more than be made up for by the chance to begin anew. As an example, "Whether we're talking about David Gardner's salary or the Department of Education and Bill Honig, the problem of our government is it's too top-heavy. Three new California governments would be cheaper than the 142-year-old layers of  bureaucracy we now have. We would get to build from the bottom up." To his credit, Statham has pushed the idea of division farther along then anyone might have expected. He has made dividing the state a credible issue. He is not Don Quixote tilting at windmills. But he does have a very long way to go. 🏛

EXECUTIVE BRANCH & BUDGET

One might think from reading the state Constitution that California's chief executive has absolute authority. In reality, California's governor has, as does the President of the United States, power that is counter-balanced by power of the other branches of government and the electorate. The governor reigns supreme in very few areas. One of them is appointments, but many of these are subject to confirmation by the state Senate. California's governor has remarkably few appointments compared to other states because the civil service system has long been established for all but the top policy posts. The governor also has prime responsibility for the fiscal affairs of state, but his budget is subject to alteration by the Legislature. The governor can reduce or eliminate items in the budget passed by the Legislature. This "line-item" veto is a very powerful tool of California Governors. These vetoes, like any others, are subject to override by two-thirds vote of the Senate and Assembly, through this happens only rarely. Former Republican Presidents Ronald Reagan and George Bush supported a line-item veto federal amendment to strengthen the executive's fiscal power. Democratic President Bill Clinton is also an admirer of the line-item veto.

Governors are elected for four-year terms, with a two-term maximum (established by Proposition 140 in November 1990). Historically, only Earl Warren was elected more than twice. The order of succession is the lieutenant governor, Senate president pro tempore, Assembly speaker, secretary of state, attorney general, treasurer and controller. The governor serves as the ceremonial chief of state, as president of the University of California Board of Regents and the State University and Colleges Board of Trustees, as unofficial leader of his party, and as the head of most administrative agencies through his subordinate appointees. The governor is deeply involved in the legislative process, through presentation of the budget, the office's veto power and the traditional presentation of a package of bills constituting a legislative program (and usually outlined in the annual "state-of-the-state" message). When stymied by the legislature, Governor Pete Wilson has also authored initiatives.

Veto power

The veto is perhaps the governors most potent weapon, but it is essentially a negative power. Governors usually wield considerable influence with members of their own party (because they often control the party structure, weak as it is, and because lawmakers like to stay on the good side of a governor so they can get projects for their districts and appointments for their friends). Consequently, vetoes are rarely overridden. When Governor Ronald Reagan had a veto overridden during the 1973-74 session, it was the first over-ride since 1946. Jerry Brown was overridden during his first term on a death-penalty measure and overrides became almost commonplace in 1979, especially on fiscal issues. Neither George Deukmejian nor Pete Wilson has had a veto overridden.

Governors have the power to organize the administrative agencies of state government as they see fit, although the Legislature can veto major reorganization plans. Reagan organized his administration into four agencies headed by the secretaries of health and welfare, business and transportation, agriculture and services, and resources. The Department of Finance reported directly to the Governor. The cabinet met regularly and established policy for the administration.

The Jerry Brown administration employed the case-study method for solving problems and establishing policies. Cabinet sessions at the start were frequent, lengthy and argumentative — far less business-like than in the Reagan years. However Brown put agency executives on a loose leash once they learned what he expected from them. Jerry Brown created a fifth agency, the Youth and Adult Correctional Agency.

George Deukmejian, it was assumed, would be willing to bargain and compromise with the legislature on issues since, as a former legislator, he was used to a give and take process. His unyielding stance during his first year in office on issues like taxes and community college fees surprised many. Despite the fact that he was the sole Republican among the state's statewide officeholders and both houses of the Legislature were Democratic-controlled, Deukmejian wielded the powers of his office with considerable effect.

Deukmejian's Republican successor, Governor Pete Wilson, selected a more moderate and pragmatic group of Cabinet secretaries. Wilson also established a sixth new cabinet and agency: environmental protection, similar to one created administratively by Deukmejian.

Sharing executive power with the governor are a

number of boards and commissions. The governor appoints most of their members and they in turn exercise independent authority. Among them:

University of California of Regents. Aside from the power of the purse, the Regents control the university system.

State University Trustees. This board has less power and prestige than the UC Regents but has been seeking increased independence.

Public Utilities Commission. The PUC sets rates for public utilities and also exercises allied responsibilities.

Franchise Tax Board. This board administers the state income tax and handles other revenue matters.

State Lands Commission. This commission exercises control over the state's oil-rich tidelands and other public properties.

Fair Political Practices Commission. This powerful agency was created by voters in June 1974 to police the state's Political Reform Act covering lobbyist activities, campaign contributions and conflicts of interest.

Energy Resources, Conservation and Development Commission. This commission also went into operation in 1975. It is charged with establishing overall state power policy and with the selection of sites for new power plants.

Agricultural Labor Relations Board. This agency supervises management-labor activities for the agricultural industry.

Lottery Commission. Created by the 1984 initiative to run what is, in effect, one of the nation's largest businesses.

Citizens Compensation Commission. This governmental unit was established by voters with the adoption of Prop. 112 of June 1990. This commission is charged with setting the salary level of all state elected officials except judges.

In a special category is the *State Board of Equalization,* composed of the state controller and four members elected by district. It collects the sales tax and other levies, and supervises county administration of the property tax. From time to time, governors propose elimination of the Board of Equalization and the Franchise Tax Board in favor of creating a Department of Revenue under the governor's control.

Statewide offices

In addition to the governor, the state Constitution requires the election of seven other statewide officials. All are limited to two four-year terms by Proposition 140 (except for the Insurance Commissioner whose office was created after the initiative was drafted). See box for a list of current incumbents, the individuals they defeated and their predecessors.

Here is a brief rundown of the duties of these other statewide officials:

• **Lieutenant Governor:** presides over the Senate, serves as a member of numerous state boards and commissions, and exercises the powers of chief executive when the governor leaves the state or is incapacitated.

• **Secretary of State:** the state's chief election officer; maintains all the state's official files and historical documents, including articles of incorporation; receives lobbyists' registrations and their monthly reports; receives campaign-contribution and conflict-of-interest disclosure forms.

• **Attorney General:** the state's chief law enforcement officer, legal advisor to state agencies.

• **Treasurer:** provides all banking services for the state, including sale of bonds and investment of securities.

• **Controller:** the principal accounting and disbursement officer for the state; administers inheritance and gift taxes and performs a variety of functions assigned by the Legislature, including publication of statistics on local government.

• **Superintendent of Public Instruction:** heads the state Department of Education, but most of the public schools are administered by local boards; state education policy is established by the state Board of Education, composed of gubernatorial appointees.

• **Insurance Commissioner:** This is a relatively new position created by the passage of Proposition 103 in 1988.

Constitutional Officers

	Incumbent (year first elected)	Defeated Nov. 1990	Predecessor
Governor	Pete Wilson (R) 1990	Dianne Feinstein (D)	George Deukmejian (R)
Lieutenant Governor	Leo T. McCarthy (D) 1982	Marian Bergeson (R)	Mike Curb (R)
Secretary of State	March Fong Eu (D) 1974	Joan Milke Flores (R)	Edmund G. Brown Jr. (D)
Attorney General	Dan Lungren (R) 1990	Arlo Smith (D)	John Van de Kamp (D)
Treasurer	Kathleen Brown (D) 1990	Tom Hayes (R)	Tom Hayes (R)
Insurance Commissioner	John Garamendi (D) 1990	Wes Bannister (R)	— none —
Controller	Gray Davis (D) 1986	Matt Fong (R)	Kenneth Cory (D)
Superintendent of Public Instruction	(nonpartisan)	Louis (Bill) Honig*	Wilson Riles

Note: Minor-party candidates omitted.   *Vacated office upon conviction of a felony March 1993

California Executive Branch Organization

Governor

Independent Commissions
Agricultural Labor Relations Board
Arts Council
Lottery Commission
State Lands Commission
Coastal Commission
Fair Political Practices Commmission
"Little Hoover" Commission
Public Employment Relations Board
Transportation Commission

Elected Constitutional Officers
Lieutenant Governor
Secretary of State
Controller
Treasurer
Board of Equalization(4)
Attorney General (Department of Justice)
Superintendent of Public Instruction
  (Department of Education)
Insurance Commissioner

Office of Adminstrative Law
Office of Planning and Research
Office of Emergency Services
Office of Economic Opportunity
Office of Personnel Administration
Military Department
Office of Criminal Justice Planning
State Public Defender

Education Policy Boards
Board of Education
U.C. Board of Regents
State College and University Trustees
Community College Board of Governors
Postsecondary Education Commission
Commission for Teacher Preparation and
  Licensing

Business, Transportation and Housing Agency
Dept. of Alcoholic Beverage
  Control
Dept. of State Banking
Dept. of Corporations
Highway Patrol
Dept. of Housing and
  Community Development
Dept. of Motor Vehicles
Dept. of Real Estate
Dept. of Savings and Loan
Dept. of Transporation
California Housing Finance
  Agency
Stephen P. Teale Data Center
Office of Traffic Safety

Resources Agency
Dept. of Conservation
Dept. of Fish and Game
Dept. of Forestry & Fire
  Protection
Dept. of Boating and
  Waterways
Dept. of Parks and Recreation
Reclamation Board
S.F. Bay Conservation and
  Development Commission
Dept. of Water Resources
California Conservation Corps
Colorado River Board
Coastal Commission

Health and Welfare Agency
Dept. of Alcohol and Drug
  Programs
Employment Development Dept.
Dept. of Developmental Services
Dept. of Health Services
Dept. of Mental Health
Dept. of Rehabilitation
Dept of Social Services
Dept. of Aging
Office of Statewide Health
  Planning and Development
Emergency Medical Services
  Authority
Health & Welfare Data Center

State and Consumer Services Agency
Fire Marshall
Franchise Tax Board
Dept. of General Services
Personnel Board
Dept. of Consumer Affairs
Public Employees'
  Retirement System
Teachers' Retirement System
Dept. of Veterans' Affairs
Dept. of Fair Employment
  and Housing
Building Standards
  Commission
Museum of Science &
  Industry

Trade and Commerce Agency
World Trade Commission
California Film Commission
Office of Tourism
Office of Small Business
  Development

Youth and Adult Correctional Agency
Board of Prison Terms
Dept. of Corrections
Board of Corrections
Prison Industries Authority
Youthful Offender Parole Baord
Dept. of Youth Authority

Environmental Protection Agency
Air Resources Board
Integrated Waste Management
  Board
Water Resources Control Board
Dept. of Toxic Substance Control
Dept. of Pesticide Regulation
Office of Environmental Helath
  Hazard Assessment

Department of Food and Agriculture

Department of Finance

Department of Industrial Relations

Secretary of Child Development & Education

The commissioner oversees the operations of the state Department of Insurance and has wide authority to approve or disapprove many types of insurance rates.

State Finance

The governor is required by the state Constitution to present a budget each January — an estimate of the state's expenditures and revenues for the fiscal year starting the following July 1st. In a state growing as fast as California, the budget increases dramatically no matter who is governor.

During the eight years Ronald Reagan was governor, the total budget doubled from $5 billion to $10 billion. Jerry Brown's first budget (1975-76) totaled $11.4 billion, and his final budget (1982-83) totaled $25.3 billion. George Deukmejian's first budget (1983-84) totaled $26.8 billion and his last budget (1990-91) was $54.4 billion. Governor Pete Wilson's first budget was $55.7 billion.

These figures can be misleading because they do not show how much the cost of state government has risen. Many of the increases were for the exclusive purpose of relieving-pressure on the property tax or on local government, especially after the passage of Proposition 13 in 1978. In fact, about two-thirds of each year's budget consists of allocations to schools and other elements of local government, and about half the state budget is for public education.

Budget process

The budget process in the Legislature involves detailed study of items that are questioned by the Legislature's fiscal specialist, the legislative analyst. For months, subcommittees of the Senate Budget and Fiscal Review Committee and the Assembly Ways and Means Committee pore over the budget and decide which items should be increased, reduced, added or eliminated. Eventually, the budget is packaged by the fiscal committees and sent to the floor of each house. As a practical matter, either the Senate or the Assembly bill becomes the vehicle for enactment of a budget. The first house to act sends its version of the bill to the other, which then puts its own figures into the legislation and sends it back to the house of origin. The changes are routinely rejected, and the budget is placed in the hands of a conference committee composed of members of both chambers. Even though the constitution requires that the budget be sent to the governor by June 15th, it is often much later before both houses are able to adopt a compromise because passage by a two-thirds majority is required.

Revenue

One major portion of the budget — estimated revenues — is not considered at all by the Legislature, except to verify that funds will be sufficient to meet anticipated expenditures. The difference between revenues and expenditures (with any carryover from the previous year taken into account) produces the projected surplus for the fiscal year.

About 77 percent of the revenue goes into the state general fund. The remaining 23 percent is collected from specific sources and placed in special funds (notably the motor vehicle fund) to be spent for specific purposes. Estimates in the governor's proposed budget for the 1993-94 fiscal year show anticipated revenue from all funds of $52 billion ($39.9 billion general fund; $12.1 billion special funds). Specific fund sources and their percent of total revenue are as follows:

Personal income tax, $16.1 billion (32.5%);
Sales tax, $14.3 billion (27.5%);
Bank & corporation taxes, $4.9 billion (9.4%);
Insurance, $1.2 billion (2.3%);
Motor vehicle (inc. gas tax), $7.2 billion (13.8%);
Tobacco, $689 million (1.3%);
Liquor, $291 million (0.6%);
Estate taxes, $608 million (1.2%);
Horse racing fees, $115 million (0.2%);
Other, $4.1 billion (7.9%).

Expenditures

Total proposed 1993-94 expenditures are $49.7 billion, not counting bond funds. Here are the major items of expenditure as proposed by the governor in January 1993:

Aid to schools K-12, $14.7 billion (29.6%);
Health and welfare, $15.4 billion (31.0%);
Higher education, $4.0 billion (8.0%);
Business, transportation and housing, $4.0 billion (8.0%);
Local government, $3.0 billion (6.0%);
Youth and adult corrections, $3.1 billion (6.2%);
Other, $5.1 billion (10.3%).

Clouding the fiscal picture in 1991-92, Governor Pete Wilson's first year as chief executive, was the unprecedented and massive deficit, which ultimately surpassed $14 billion. A deficit of nearly $12 billion had to be dealt with for 1992-93, and the anticipated deficit for 1993-94 ranged in excess of $8 billion.

While the Legislature can revise the budget in any way it sees fit, the governor has only two choices when he receives the bill act at the end of June: he can veto it in its entirety and thus force the Legislature to pass a new bill, or he can reduce and eliminate specific items (this is known as blue-penciling the budget through line-item veto). This latter is the practice traditionally used.

Until the budget is enacted, the Legislature cannot pass appropriations measures unless the governor provides a letter saying that the expenditure is needed on an emergency basis. Once the budget is passed, however, the Legislature can — and usually does — send the governor numerous bills containing appropriations. The governor can cut the entire appropriation or reduce the amount. (Each of these bills can contain only a single appropriation.) 🏛

Pete Wilson:

Steering through a sea of woes

By Richard Zeiger

photos by Rich Pedroncelli

Reprinted from *California Journal*, April 1992

PETE WILSON IS WEARING THE SHEEPISH LOOK he gets when engaged in an activity that may not be dignified enough for the governor of the nation's largest state. He is about to tack a sign to his office door saying, "No Smoking." The effort, accompanied by a raft of television cameras, is to publicize his new executive order banning smoking from all state office buildings. The event is of dubious significance, since most state departments had already eliminat ed smoking and the most prominent exception, the state Capitol itself, is under the control of the Legislature and thus outside of Wilson's domain.

But if the action will have less than cosmic significance, it does succeed in one major respect: It gets Wilson a few precious moments on television news.

Indeed, the Wilson handlers are so enchanted with the motif that they repeat it several days later when Wilson proclaims the official end of the state's six-year drought by posting a new sign over the drought-emergency office, identifying it now as the water-conservation office. Wilson stages the event despite the fact that a day earlier, by mistake, bureaucrats within the state had confessed that the drought had indeed ended, thus stealing their boss' thunder. No matter; the television cameras roll again.

Welcome to the start of Pete Wilson's 1994 re-election campaign.

There has been no formal announcement, of course, but Wilson concedes, "I suppose we have been a little bit more visible."

Although it may seem a trifle premature to be campaigning with the election 20 months away, Pete Wilson has a very long way to go. Indeed, there are many who believe it is all but impossible for Wilson to win a second term, which would make him the first one-term California governor in more than 50 years. Culbert Olson managed it by losing to Earl Warren in 1942.

But Wilson's standings in the public opinion polls remain at an all-time low despite a recent upturn. With the state's economy stubbornly refusing to rebound and with

prospects good for another budget crisis this summer, it could take an extraordinary change of luck for Wilson to survive. And so far, just about all of Wilson's luck has been bad. As governor, he has been faced with a series of natural and man-made disasters of biblical proportions: fires, earthquakes, drought, floods and even urban rioting.

To make matters worse, the national recession and post-cold war cutback in military spending have hit the state with a fury unknown since the Great Depression. In the post-Proposition 13 era, the state's revenue stream has become unusually sensitive to changes in the economy. The property tax is fairly stable even in bad economic times, but the sales and income taxes — the state's major sources of money — fall off rapidly in bad economic times, and Wilson and the state Legislature have been faced with one intractable budget deficit after another.

And chances are good that the same thing might happen again. Democrats and Republicans remain far apart on key issues. Wilson hopes that the new freshman class will be more receptive to making what he describes as the "necessary tough decisions." But some early Wilson deadlines for budget cuts have come and gone, and so far there has been no indication that the new Legislature is any more willing to bend to the Wilson will than was the old one.

Wilson agrees that "in one sense" he has been the victim of bad luck. But the circumstances of his first term, and his reaction to them, have left him "with a story to tell. When it's told and people begin to appreciate it and think about it they will come to the same conclusion: That in fact it's been a time of unrelenting challenges of all kinds and that they have indeed been tough times but they've been met pretty well."

"You have to be aggressive about getting the story out. That is what we haven't done," Wilson said in an interview with *California Journal.*

But if the times were difficult, Wilson's response hasn't always been consistent. In his first year, to deal with the deficit by cutting a deal with legislative Democrats, he accepted substantial increases in taxes and, in exchange, Democrats agreed to some cuts in programs. But portions of the deal also were cobbled together with questionable fiscal gimmicks, and the budget began to unravel before the year was out. Moreover, the conservative faction in Wilson's own party, never really fans of Wilson's to begin with, were angered further by the tax increases. When Wilson's first year ended, the governor seemingly was without a friend in the world.

The second year was not much better. Wilson decided there was little political or practical advantage in combining with Democrats on the budget, and that the worsening financial situation made it impossible and inadvisable to try and balance the budget with more taxes. So Wilson hunkered down. He had learned the lesson that the governor who is willing to say "no" to the Legislature can have the upper hand. Wilson for the most part refused to parley with legislative Democrats, and this led to a budget impasse that lasted more than two months but that was largely settled on Wilson's terms.

"What I understand very well is that while the public is inclined to say, 'A plague on both your houses,' the Legislature is an abstraction to them. They never connect that good old Charlie that they keep re-electing is part of the problem. By contrast, the governor . . . is almost by definition high-profile. If they're not happy with something, he's likely to get a major share of the credit," Wilson offered.

Democrats, he maintained, were willing to hold up the budget in order to gain political advantage. "They haven't even been subtle about it. The speaker [Willie Brown] even indicated in a *New York Times* profile on me . . . it was his purpose to deny me re-election."

But in saying now that he always knew he would get the worst end of a budget impasse, Wilson is indulging in a little revisionist history. At the time, the administration thought that Wilson was in the better position to sit out the

storm. After all, it was the legislators, mostly Democrats, who were up for election in November 1992. The governor wouldn't have to face voters for more than two years. By that time, these budget difficulties would surely be history.

An election debacle
∽⟆⟅∾

Things didn't quite work that way. The '92 budget fracas was followed by November elections that gave Democrats a resounding victory. They captured both seats in the U.S. Senate, including Wilson's old Senate seat with a victory over John Seymour — Wilson's hand-picked successor; secured the state's electoral votes for Bill Clinton; gained a seat in the state Assembly despite a new reapportionment plan drawn by the state Supreme Court that was expected to benefit Republicans; and managed to defeat Wilson's initiative measure to cut welfare spending while increasing his own powers as chief executive.

All-in-all, it was a dismal showing for Wilson and added to the notion that his re-election prospects are dubious. There was even some talk that he might be subject to a challenge from within his own party. The names of a few conservative challengers were floated, including that of Bay Buchanan, an unsuccessful primary contestant for state treasurer in 1990 and the sister of erstwhile columnist and presidential candidate Pat Buchanan, and that of former Assemblyman Tom McClintock, who

A recent round of base closures added to Wilson's woes

seems to be in favor despite the fact that he was defeated in a 1992 bid for Congress.

Most of that talk died down following last month's Republican state convention as the GOP came to realize that, if it wasn't in love with Wilson, it did like controlling the governor's office.

"When you've lost the White House and you find your governor down 16 points in the Field Poll, it reminds you of why you need to stick together," notes Republican consultant Sal Russo.

But even if Wilson manages to avoid a strong challenge from within his own party, he won't be so lucky in the general election. The Democrats have an array of candidates available to challenge Wilson, and polls at this point show them beating the incumbent.

The favorite of the political cognoscenti at the moment is state Treasurer Kathleen Brown. The daughter of former Governor Pat Brown and the sister of former Governor Jerry Brown, Kathleen already has put more than $2 million in the bank that could be the start of a run for governor. In addition, during the 1992 elections, she campaigned tirelessly for an array of Democrats, assistance that should be repaid in 1994 if she decides to run. Brown possesses the charm of her father and the intelligence of her brother and, at least so far, has not displayed the drawbacks of either.

However, Wilson supporters say that can't last forever.

"Kathleen Brown is an unknown commodity. The more she's known, the less strong she becomes," offers Republican consultant Ray McNally. "Kathleen Brown has nowhere to go but down, and Pete Wilson has nowhere to go but up. It's dangerous to predict Pete Wilson is a one-term governor."

Kathleen Brown has nowhere to go but down, and Pete Wilson has nowhere to go but up. It's dangerous to predict Pete Wilson is a one-term governor.

In addition, the Wilson crew says that Brown isn't well-known to the public. As voters get to know her better, chances are many will not like what they see, particularly if they have some help from a Wilson campaign. They also scorn Brown for what they claim is her failure to take a stand on tough issues.

"Take the sales-tax extension. She says it should be firmly on the table for discussion. There's a tough position," notes Wilson communications director Dan Schnur.

Furthermore, Brown still must make it through a presumably contested primary. Her most likely opponent is state Insurance Commissioner John Garamendi. Also bright and attractive, Garamendi was the titular head of Bill Clinton's California campaign. Even so, Garamendi probably has fewer chits for 1994. For one thing, Garamendi used up some of his capital trying to win his wife, Patty, a seat in Congress. She lost, in her third try for public office, and that defeat may have included the added burden of hobbling her husband's bid for advancement.

Also a long-shot to run is Controller Gray Davis. Davis tried to beat Dianne Feinstein for the U.S. Senate nomination in 1990 and a nasty turn toward the end of that campaign made him unpopular with some Democrats.

The award for the most whimsical proposal floated so far, though, must go to those who are advancing Willie Brown as a candidate for governor. Although certainly bright and knowledgeable about state government — a person certainly qualified to serve — Brown probably is not electable. Over the years, rightly or wrongly, he has shouldered the burden for all of the complaints about the ineptness of California's Legislature. He has some of the highest negative ratings of any California elected official. Even if he could win a Democratic primary, chances are very slim he would win in November. Brown knows this and has done nothing to encourage the trial balloons. But the mere mention has been enough to set off a load of quips, including one GOP stalwart who offered that if Willie Brown should get the Democratic nomination, it was "proof that God is a Republican."

But the Almighty rarely makes such blatant interventions in the affairs of mankind, and Wilson likely will face much more formidable opposition.

And Wilson is no pushover. Beneath a placid exterior is a rock-hard campaigner; the Marine who refuses to know when he's licked.

"He's determined and very proud. And he's often underestimated. He welcomes the fact that he'll be judged an easy mark," notes Larry Thomas, a Wilson confidant who worked for the governor when he was still mayor of San Diego. Plus, said Thomas, there are the "inherent powers of the office that can be used to achieve goals and to capture the public attention. He's a man who's skilled at doing that, particularly if he get a little running room from the problems that have been plaguing the state."

Wilson has also been making staff changes, and observers now believe that he has a team in place that is up to the re-election challenge. Indeed, staff difficulties in the beginning of Wilson's administration have been cited as the cause of some of the governor's problems.

"I don't think he's been well-served," notes one Republican observer, who asked to remain anonymous. "He's got some fine people, but by and large, there have been too many screw-ups."

Wilson brought in George Dunn and Joe Shumate and deputy chiefs of staff, as well as Republican hit-man Joe Rodota to be his cabinet secretary. Furthermore, Schnur has hit his stride as Wilson's chief spokesman, a task that had been conspicuously missing after the untimely death in 1991 of Wilson confidant Otto Bos.

Wilson also has refined his position on the economic front. No more finding the middle road that characterized his first year. Now Wilson's mantra is that the state must do all it can to create jobs in the private sector. That means changing the worker's compensation system and giving tax breaks to industry. And it means that a long-awaited Wilson proposal on managing growth in the state turned out to be a tepid rehash of existing policies along with a plea for streamlining the state's various permit processes so that growth can continue. Indeed, there are even some in the environmental community, where Wilson has long been considered one of the few reliable Republicans, who believe the governor is now willing to soften state environmental laws if it will spur business development.

Wilson's own personality should also be given some of the blame. Wilson is good at standing firm, but such a position makes one inflexible. And when events don't go as you plan — as they have not in the first two years of the Wilson administration — a little flexibility might be useful.

Events have forced Wilson to be a governor playing defense. That's not what he had in mind when he got elected. Wilson came to office promising to be one of the most active governors in recent state history. His program of preventive care for children of all economic stripes was novel and aggressive. Indeed, his was the notion that every child should have a "mentor" to help him or her get through the difficult business of growing up. The concept that government would help find everyone a guardian, at its core, can be considered very un-Republican, but Wilson doesn't see it that way.

"The kinds of things that are necessary to give kids the best break in life include those things that are governmental programs like health care for poor mothers, pre-natal care . . . and the entire range of early childhood programs we have instituted," says Wilson. "There has to be an individual, some individual to get them off in life and really to carry them on through."

"I don't think it's a partisan activity," Wilson

notes. Lots of volunteer groups already are in the business, and government should be supporting these. "There are hundreds of organizations like this and there should be more."

But the budget crisis has kept Wilson from all but a token start to his new programs; a promise that, one day, things might get better. But for now, Wilson has been the unluckiest of recent governors, and now it just could take a substantial change in fortune for him to survive, although Wilson doesn't see it that way.

"It's easy to govern in easy times."

"I'm not counting on that," Wilson said. "You make your own luck. People do win re-election who had re-elect negatives that caused people to write them off. Those things change when you have someone to run against.

"It's easy to govern in easy times. It's difficult to govern in difficult times. You are probably a better governor when you are compelled to manage well and lead in difficult times. It's a hell of a lot more difficult to do.

"The best way to run for any office . . . is to simply do the best job possible with the one you've got. That's what gives you the greatest credibility. Talk is cheap. It is very easy to make promises and it is very difficult for people to judge; they may want to believe the promises but in fact what is most credible to them is what should be — what you've actually done." 🏛

Budget negotiations with legislative leaders mostly produced gridlock in 1992

Is California driving business out of the state?

By Mary Beth Barber

Reprinted from *California Journal*, May 1993

FOR MORE THAN A century, California has been the state where dreams were made. Some dreams were grand: striking it rich in the Sierra Nevada gold fields or on Hollywood's silver screen. Most were modest: a steady job, a house in the suburbs with a patch of lawn and two cars in the garage.

But California's golden sheen has tarnished in recent years. The economic giant that snickered at the economic slides of less-favored parts of the nation has had its comeuppance. And, as the saying goes. The bigger they are, the harder they fall.

Construction, once a booming industry, has declined as residents refuse to chance buying a home during bad economic times. Aerospace manufacturers, who got rich during the defense build-ups of the Reagan years, have been forced to change with the end of the Cold War and downsize or develop new products. Small businesses surrounding closed or soon-to-be-closed military installations are struggling to gain customers. And large manufacturing companies have been expanding or moving to other states.

Word in business circles: Unload California.

Question from state officials: Why?

California has never been a state to directly woo business. It never had to. Government spending during World War II, particularly in the aircraft and ship-building industries, abounded in the state. After World War II, Northern California was the birthplace of the computer industry; Southern California supplied

illustration by Pierre Babasin

entertainment for the populace and high-tech weaponry for the federal government. The education system, universities, highly trained workforce, large markets and high quality of life created a situation where California didn't come looking for business —business came looking for California.

"For years we took the Club Med approach of 'You're lucky we let you on the trip,'" said state Controller Gray Davis at a seminar at the University of California, Davis.

Despite that attitude, many companies still chose to start and grow here. Now, however, some businesses are choosing to move or expand elsewhere, such as the silicon-chip manufacturing giant Intel. New Mexico is home to a new Intel manufacturing facility that will employ 1000 people. "What's changed," said Intel spokesman Richard Hall, "is that California has become less competitive while other states have become more competitive."

Business groups and politicians say the Intel experience is typical of what is happening in California. The state's problems are just so great, and most businesses don't want to face them. The state has layered regulation on top of regulation. The cost of wages remains high, but the quality of workers has dropped. The workers compensation system is a mess. And other states are more than willing to offer incentives to new businesses. New Mexico, for example, offered Intel $114 million in tax incentives and job-training funds. Firms that have the choice simply find it cheaper to operate elsewhere.

Governor Pete Wilson, business groups and some politicians citing the negative business climate say the state is losing jobs hand-over-fist. They are using the claim to justify an array of pro-business changes in state law that include everything from easing environmental regulations to granting tax breaks to companies. Faced with high unemployment, the budget crisis and the recession, politicians from both parties have acknowledged that the state has to do something.

The first question that needs to be asked, however, is whether jobs are actually leaving the state or whether California is experiencing a natural economic downswing felt in the rest of the country during the middle and late 1980s. According to a December 1991 study released by the Center for Continuing Study of the California Economy, a Palo Alto-based group, the state's job losses have been caused by the recession and not by a business exodus to other states. Other experts agree.

"No more than 5 to 10 percent of job losses in this state have been due to out-migration of business," said Tapan Munroe, chief economist for Pacific Gas and Electric, to the California Economic Summit organized by Speaker Willie Brown and held in Los Angeles this past February.

But an analysis based on the "California Migration Study," conducted by California's largest utilities, indicates that California's manufacturing industry has decreased. The study said that 708 manufacturing plants relo-

cated or chose to expand outside of California between 1987 and 1992, taking with them 107,000 jobs. Furthermore, an even larger number of manufacturing jobs simply disappeared as businesses closed or cut back during the recession. Similar jobs have not replaced the lost ones. Manufacturing jobs in the state — as a percentage of the total workforce — decreased between 1979 and 1989, said California Manufacturers Association spokesman Bill George.

Instead, most of the jobs are being replaced by service-oriented industries, positions that don't pay workers nearly as well. According to the utilities' industry migration study, "Seventy-three percent of manufacturing job losses are in industries with wages above the average for California's total private sector employment." Many of the low-wage manufacturing jobs were lost to Mexico; the other losses were the result of defense cutbacks and out-of-state migration.

The downsizing of the aerospace industry, one of the largest manufacturing employers in Southern California, is beginning to look even worse than previously imagined. Companies that have to shrink are faced with tough decisions about where to consolidate. Hughes Aircraft announced in March that it will move its engineering facilities from Canoga Park to Tucson. California's negative business climate and government's inability to solve problems were factors in the decision. Northrop. may be in a similar situation in the near future, said corporate vice president Marvin Elkin.

All is not gloom-and-doom, how-

ever. Barry Sedlik, a manager with Southern California Edison and principal co-author of the utilities' migration study, explained at the UC Davis seminar that some manufacturing sectors could prove to be profitable for the state, especially for Southern California. The electric vehicle, rail car and apparel industries could flourish in the Los Angeles area, he said.

While there is room for other industries to move into California, it will take time and capital for them to grow. Optimists believe the engineers and manufacturing employees that were once aerospace workers can switch their expertise to ground transportation. Some of the skills cross-apply, but expecting all displaced aerospace workers to find employment in these new fields is unrealistic, according to the Economic Roundtable of Southern California. The organization found that the aerospace workers wishing to work on rail-car manufacturing would experience a loss of wages, and this industry can't possibly take up all the slack. Electric cars could become a viable alternative, but the industry is as yet too young.

The answer right now is to maintain current industries in the state and attract businesses from elsewhere. Many companies don't even consider California as a place to start or expand, and California must take steps to change that attitude. Without industries to replace the high-paying manufacturing jobs, California may be stuck in this recession for years to come.

But knowing just what businesses want from the state, and finding the capacity to provide it, turns out to be

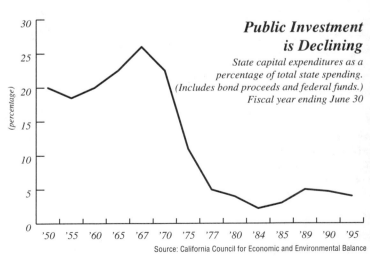

Public Investment is Declining

State capital expenditures as a percentage of total state spending. (Includes bond proceeds and federal funds.) Fiscal year ending June 30

Source: California Council for Economic and Environmental Balance

a tricky proposition.

Companies that responded to the utilities' study cited labor, worker's compensation costs, taxes and other economic disincentives as major factors for leaving the state. Environmental regulations also pose a significant problem — not the standards themselves, but the manner in which they are handled by the myriad of state and local agencies.Even when businesses want to cooperate, they find the maze of regulations almost impossible to satisfy.

M ost businesses have no problems with high standards, said Elkin. After all, their employees have to breathe the air and drink the water, too. But when a simple change to their operations must be reviewed by a half-dozen agencies and takes months to complete, other states' more simple regulations seem a lot more appealing.

Worker's compensation is another area where the grass looks greener on the other side of the state line. Just about every other state has problems with the workers compensation system, but none seem as apparent as California's. Businesses here pay among the highest insurance premiums, but injured workers receive the lowest awards. While larger businesses see this only as a minor problem — most are self-insured — small business claims the high rates are crushing them.

The state's problems aren't necessarily new but have become more apparent during the bad economic times. The '80s were good to business in California, said CMA's George, and few companies or groups paid attention to minor rises in worker's compensation rates or new regulations. Now that times are bad, what used to be minor costs add up and may be the difference between being in the red or the black.

Part of the blame can be placed on the Legislature, George continued. Industry wasn't looking closely enough when Sacramento got caught up in what he calls the "good-idea movement." One legislator would have a good idea and pass a law, often with industry's approval. "Then other legislators would expand on that idea," he said, and create a myriad of regulations that ultimately did more harm then good, such as gross over-regulation and a worker's compensation sys-

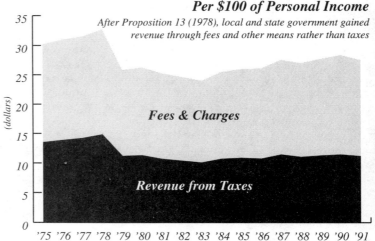

California State and Local Own-Source Revenues Per $100 of Personal Income

After Proposition 13 (1978), local and state government gained revenue through fees and other means rather than taxes

Fees & Charges

Revenue from Taxes

Source: U.S. Department of Commerce, Bureau of the Census and from the Governor's Budget, California Statistical Abstract, and Dept. of Finance

tem that "is way too liberal."

"A lot of it is the business community's fault," said George. "They signed off. When companies are making money, worker's compensation costs and fees are no big deal."

With re-election around the corner and the state's economy showing no signs of recovery, Wilson has made the courting of business a top priority. Julie Meier Wright, secretary of the Trade and Commerce Agency, said that worker's compensation reform should be a top priority, along with changing the law to make it more difficult to sue business for things such as product liability questions. Businesses find themselves faced with endless delays because of lawsuits brought on by special-interest groups, she said. "Quite often a lawsuit doesn't have to be viable, it just has to be enough to delay the project, which is of course winning."

The proposed low-level radioactive waste facility in the Mojave Desert area of Ward Valley is a key example of a project delay from lawsuits. The state, under federal regulations, was required to have a working facility by the beginning of this year. That deadline has come and gone, and construction on the facility hasn't even begun because of a series of lawsuits dealing with the permit process, public hearings and the Endangered Species Act. Bio-tech firms may move to other states such as Nevada that have such disposal facilities, said Wilson spokeswoman Kassy Perry.

Regulatory reform has been one of Wilson's top priorities since coming into office in 1991. One of his first moves as governor was to create the

California Environmental Protection Agency, an umbrella agency that oversees many of the departments that issue permits. Led by Secretary James Strock, previously the head of enforcement for the federal EPA, Cal/EPA set out to streamline the regulatory process without interfering with California's long tradition of high standards.

"There has been a myth perpetuated in California that somehow high standards require a long permitting process," said Strock. "That's not written in stone."

Environmentalists, however, charge that Cal/EPA has overlooked essential environmental protection in its efforts to make things easier for business. Strock flatly denied the allegations. "The fundamental goal of the agency is for the environment," he said.

The environmentalists are right on one point, however. Strock said that he has met industry representatives who claim to be complaining about the large number of permits mandated, when they are really challenging the standards set by the Legislature. "We stay out of arguments that are misleading," said Strock.

Some businesses don't see Cal/EPA helping unburden the regulatory process, however. "There's just another layer of bureaucracy that has been created," said one industry leader. Unlike the single-agency federal EPA, Cal/EPA is an umbrella agency overseeing many boards and departments. All permits must go to the separate boards *and* to Cal/EPA now. "To their credit, I think they are trying," he said of the agency.

While many business interests point to particular parts of state and local government as the problem, the California Council for Economic and Environmental Balance (CCEEB), a group financed primarily by the state's large industries, says the problems are more fundamental to how the state runs itself now versus 20 years ago. California has ceased to spend money on itself, said CCEEB Vice President Lisa Bicker. "For the past 20 years, we have been living off the investments we made twenty years ago," she said.

The incredible success during the '60s and '70s was a direct result of the investments the state made, especially at the local level. But when Proposition 13 — the initiative that capped property taxes — took effect in 1978, local governments lost a means of gaining revenue. Compounding the problem was a provision in the initiative that required a two-thirds vote for local bond measures rather than a simple majority, making bond measures almost impossible to approve. "Prop 13 took away the ability for local governments to tax themselves, to generate revenue for themselves," said Bicker. The result has been a dramatic decrease in investment spending on the local level.

The state also has spent less on investment in recent years. State capital expenditures plummeted from 25 percent of the total state budget in the early '70s to less than 5 percent by 1980 (see chart, page 11). Both state and local revenues dropped approximately 20 percent between 1978 and 1979 when Proposition 13 went into effect. And the state has been giving local governments less and less. In order to make up for these differences, local governments either had to cut programs or figure out alternative ways to gain revenue, mostly by fees. Water, sewage and garbage fees are commonplace now, as are fees for capital improvements such as sidewalks.

Overall, investment in California has decreased. The state needs new roads, sewers, schools, public transportation systems and water projects — as well as social investments such as education and child care. "We need to invest in both social and physical projects to really do anything," said Bicker.

Investment in the state's infrastructure affects the general business climate. Intel spokesman Richard Hall said that California local governments and communities in Northern California were the best to their company compared to local governments in other states. Companies, especially high-tech ones, want quality education and an educated workforce. The university system is still one of the best in the world, but recent cuts may affect the quality of research and education in the future.

Education in general looks very bleak in the state. "Whether we like it or not, there are statistics that show that children don't have a classroom to go to," said Bicker.

Other states have been able to offer these things that California used to have a monopoly on — such as high educational standards, good roads and highways, and a general high quality of life — for a fraction of the cost.

One solution is an infrastructure bank, a structure that would provide a mechanism for the state to control growth while supporting business. The bank would provide low-interest loans for construction companies that complied with state growth-management policies; companies would get a break by building plants or homes in just the right place. Companies could choose to build elsewhere, but few would, contended Bicker. "Nobody has any money, and they're not going to build without the loans."

The idea has been supported by CCEEB, environmentalists and two studies produced by the state. But providing loans and tax incentives to business can be expensive for California, especially in light of last year's budget crisis. The state is caught in a financial Catch-22. Government collects less money in tax revenues when the economy sags, but needs money to create incentives for business to get the state on its feet again. Alternatives are few, but the most obvious is a general, temporary tax such as the sales-tax increase last year.

Wilson vehemently opposes the extension, and few industry groups will outright endorse it. But the sentiment in the business community is not against it either. Bill Campbell, a former state senator who now serves as president of CMA, said that if business tax incentives cost the state too much money, an increase on the general sales tax could be a viable alternative, if absolutely necessary. Allen Zaremberg of the California Chamber of Commerce pointed to a Chamber poll showing that small businesses were affected little by the one-half cent sales tax in 1992. Only 17 percent said that the tax hurt their business. Neither organization has officially endorsed or opposed the sales-tax increase extension.

Things aren't all bleak for California. The Legislature seems to have gotten the message that the state needs to attract business. Reports published last year from both the Republicans and Democrats agreed on how to improve the state's business climate. There are signs that some bills will receive bipartisan agreement as Democrats carry bills for business groups — including Speaker Willie Brown for the California Manufacturing Association.

Workers compensation is a hot topic for legislators, and one industry spokesman was confident that some reform may take place this year. Assembly Democrat Steve Peace from Chula Vista, chairman of the Finance and Insurance Committee, proposed an all-encompassing workers compensation bill (AB 110). The bill is sponsored by the committee rather than one legislator in the hopes of receiving bipartisan support.

The state also has taken some steps. Los Angeles has a "one-stop shop" for small business permits to help rebuild the city after last year's riots. Cal/EPA officials are looking for other areas of the state to begin similar pilot projects. The Trade and Commerce Agency has set up "Red Teams" to help attract businesses to California. State and local government officials put together incentive packages to attract both large and small businesses, said a spokesman.

California has some inherent advantages. The quality of life is still very high. The state's location on the Pacific rim is ideal for exporters. California's higher education attracts scientists and academics from all over the world. And the state is an attractive place to live for foreign investors or multicultural companies because of its ethnic diversity, said Intel spokesman Hall. "If the state Legislature follows through from both sides, California could be on very competitive footing once again," Hall said. 🏛

Reprinted from *California Journal*, November 1992

A special session to nowhere

Workers' compensation gets no reform

By Tupper Hull

On any day in Southern California, on the gritty streets outside state unemployment offices, a giant, shameful hustle is played out over and over again. Workers, many recent victims of a seriously ill economy and many who speak little or no English, are invited to join with a cadre of unscrupulous doctors and lawyers to scam the state's workers' compensation insurance system.

Elsewhere, in tawdry newspaper advertisements and on cable television stations, workers are enticed into the scam. Stress on the job? Fired? Laid off? Call 1-800-MONEY-4-U.

When a worker bites, when he succumbs to the cajoling of a sidewalk capper or the authoritative voice of a television appeal, he or she enters into a murky underwold of subtle deceit and fraud. But for the small lies and vague twists of truth, the worker gets a paltry sum compared to the billions of dollars sucked out of the system by the doctors and lawyers who have benefited most from the broken and corrupt state workers' compensation insurance system.

Designed 75 years ago as a no-fault system to compensate workers injured

Tupper Hull is a Capitol correspondent for the San Francisco Examiner.

on the job, California's workers' compensation insurance system has become a grotesquely bloated, inefficient boondoggle that is one of the costliest in the United States and pays some of the most meager benefits.

On average, California employers who buy commerical workers' compensation insurance pay less than $4 for every $100 of their payroll — fifth highest in the nation. (Approximately 56 percent of the state's 600,000 employers buy workers' compensation insurance from the 300 commercial carriers who write such policies in California. Another 19 percent purchase insurance from a state fund. The remaining 25 percent, most of them large companies, are self-insured.)

But insurance premiums are tailored to specific job categories and linked to the safety record of individual companies. Some employers, therefore, are paying workers' compensaton insurance premiums that approach half their entire payroll. It is a burden the state's employer and business community says is killing them. When coupled with their other woes — the deepest and longest recession since the Depression, the near collapse of an overheated real estate market, and defense industry layoffs that will be a permanent loss to the state's economy — increasingly panicked employers say unless the state takes quick and drastic steps, workers' compensation may be the instrument of California's economic demise.

At the same time, whom the system was intended to help are only slightly better served than are employers.

The present system was created between 1911 and 1917, when workers and employers agreed it was in neither's interest for every disputed workplace injury to end up in court before a judge or jury. In exchange for giving up their rights to sue for tort, workers got a system with fixed benefits, run by bureaucrats who by a stated doctrine of law called "liberal construction" were supposed to give them the benefit of the doubt on close calls.

Today, the system has become slow-moving and unresponsive. And the benefits it pays to workers — a maximum of $148 per week for a permanent disability and $336 per week for a temporary disability — are among the lowest in the nation. Depending on how they are measured, benefits here are either the 35th lowest, according to the Association of Insurance Companies, or the 44th lowest, according to Governor Pete Wilson.

In addition to disability payments, the system pays for medical treatments for injuries suffered at the workplace and for vocational rehabilitation counseling and training.

It's difficult to find anyone who will say anything nice about the system. Wilson, in a recent radio address, called it "something that everyone agrees is broken — our state's fraud-ridden workers' compensation system."

"Workers comp has become little more than an organized scam for avaricious exploiters" is how the *Los Angeles Times* described the system.

A special competitive commission headed by former baseball commissioner Peter Ueberroth called workers' compensation a key component in the efficient job-killing machine California has created over the past quarter century.

Even Democrats, who have resisted changes in the system for fear they will end up costing workers, now concede it is in dire need of a major overhaul.

With opinions so uniform on the nature of the problem, why is the cure so elusive? Few issues have proved so vexing

for the Legislature, so resistent to compromise, so vaccinated against the pressures of public opinion.

The reason is simple: Money. Very big money.

Doctors, lawyers, insurance companies and labor unions — the biggest players on Calfornia's political horizon — all have a major stake in the present system.

Doctors who treated injured workers received 19 percent of the $11 billion spent on workers compensation in 1990, or slightly more than $2 billion, according to an insurance industry study. Hospitals and clinics, many of them owned by doctors, got another 10 percent of the pie, about $1.1 billion. Doctors who prepared reports on the degree and cause of injuries used during litigation over workers' compensation claims got another $308 million.

Workers, for whom the system was created, got 29.5 percent or slightly more than $3.2 billion. Of that, $1.5 billion was paid in permanent partial disability benefits and $1.2 billion was paid to workers who suffered temporary disability. Another $407 million, 3.7 percent of the workers' compensaton pie, was paid to train injured workers for alternative occupations, and $165 million was paid in death and permanent total disability benefits.

Insurance companies pulled $3.1 billion out of the system in overhead, profits, taxes and lawyer fees.

They all want reform — at someone else's expense. Individually, their campaign contributions have bought enough muscle to block most reforms they fear will kink their pipeline to the $11 billion workers' compensation system. When one or more of them join forces in a temporary alliance, they are unbeatable.

The California Medical Association's political action committee contributed $757,000 to legislative candidates during this year's primary election, more than any other PAC, according to the secretary of state.

"The money in this system is hemorrhaging into special interest pockets," says Michael Marks, a San Francisco lawyer who represents employers and insurance companies in workers' comepensation lawsuits.

"The Legislature can't deal with this issue because true reform would gore everybody's ox to some degree," said Ruth Holton of California Common Cause.

Within this context, Governor Wilson has waged an unrelenting, two-year campaign to change the myriad laws and regulations governing workers' compensation and the huge bureauacracy attached to it. He has shrewdly fueled the business community's anxieties about the state's economy into a kind of single-minded hatred of the present workers' compensation system. When he called state lawmakers into special session October 8th and 9th, he made no attempt to conceal his strategy. He hoped to use the hot-house pressures of an approaching election and the uncertainty of legislative districts recently altered dramatically by reapportionment to force Democrats to abandon their historic friends and supporters — labor and trial lawyers — and approve his reforms.

Indeed, in the sort of in-your-face manner that has come to characterize Pete Wilson's relationships with the Legislature, Wilson presented lawmakers with a complex package of reform proposals he said he wanted adopted without change or committee hearings. Either change workers' compensation his way or he would do his best to change the

the makeup of the Legislature. It was the kind of brute-force tactic that worked for him during the battle to redraw legislative districts and during the two-month-long budget battle.

"This guy has nerves of steel," said GOP Assemblyman B.T. Collins.

Yet this time it didn't work. Like some giant Rube Goldberg machine, Wilson's special session generated a lot of heat and wild motion but produced little. It ground to a halt after Democrats made substantial changes to Wilson's plan. Wilson, two hours before the Assembly was scheduled to open debate on the amended plan, said he would veto it. He was not interested in seeing the compromise plan or in waiting for the Senate to make its changes. Assembly Speaker Willie Brown said Wilson's unprecedented veto threat proved the governor was never serious about reform and that his true agenda was nothing more than political guerrilla theater intended to embarrass Democrats one month before Election Day.

Indeed, Democrats noted Wilson didn't even bother to stay in town for the crucial second day of the special session. He spent the day in Los Angeles, kicking off a bilingual campaign against drunk driving and attending a fund-raiser for GOP Senate candidate Bruce Herschensohn.

But the session did force an intensive and exhaustive look at workers' compensation for those lawmakers, lobbyists, and others with enough stamina to sit through the crash course. What it showed, to the surprise of some of the businessmen and women who had come to the Capitol in support of the governor, was that Wilson's plan treated doctors and insurance companies far more favorably than it treated employers. It showed that for all his tough talk about special interests, Wilson had made sure the special interests that had supported *him* were taken care of.

Under the governor's plan, insurance companies would have been able to add surcharges of any amount to employers' premiums at any time. It would have eliminated the insurance commissioner's authority to regulate those surcharges and, despite his pledge to repeal existing law guaranteeing insurers a fixed rate of return, would have replaced that law with another rate system that, in the view of some experts, would have favored insurers.

A nd this was the proposal Wilson demanded legislators adopt without change, the plan he said he would not negotiate, the bill he insisted needed no legislative hearings. During one telling moment, a business owner who had traveled to Sacramento to demand passage of the governor's plan, after sitting through hours of testimony before the Assembly Insurance Committee, said he was glad for the hearings. He had learned much from the process, he told lawmakers, and he thanked them for their efforts.

Another businessman stalked angrily from the hearing room after telling lawmakers he would never return to the Capitol to make his voice heard. "I won't be a part of this anymore. I'm tired of being used as a pawn by doctors, lawyers and insurance companies," he said.

Said Democratic Assemblyman Steve Peace of Chula Vista, "This is the best job of snookering the employers of California the insurance industry has ever done."

Wilson's plan specifically exempted law enforcement — another group of generous financial supporters — from tough restrictions he wanted imposed on stress claims. This despite the fact cities and counties say easy-to-obtain stress benefits claimed by policemen, firemen and paramedics are among their most difficult costs to control. And the plan was far kinder to doctors than had been earlier proposals. It gave doctors considerable leeway to charge fees that exceed the system's limits, and it imposed weakened restrictions on self-referrals that the powerful California Medical Association found acceptable.

Wilson's plan was anathema to organized labor, which has never supported him. It would have done away with the liberal-construction doctrine, one of the key concessions labor won when it agreed to buy into the workers' compensation system 75 years ago. It would have made it much harder for workers to qualify for benefits and would have required in many instances that they obtain medical treatment from doctors selected by employers. It also would have made it vastly more difficult for workers to obtain benefits for a wide range of occupational illnesses such as those produced by stress or caused by exposure to toxics.

But perhaps most troubling to workers and their supporters in the Legislature was Wilson's scheme to increase weekly benefits only after employers had received a verifiable reduction in gross premiums of $1 billion. That provision was the plan's poison pill. Democrats would never support such a scheme. There were too many ways to hide the genuine savings the plan was likely to generate. An insurance company that found itself paying less in claims could simply increase its dividends to stockholders or find some other way to increase its overhead expenses.

Worse, if the economy improved and companies began expanding their workforces — if workers' compensation was truly the drag on economic recovery that Wilson claims — the total amount paid in premiums would rise, not drop. Why should workers, who already have given up their rights to sue their employers, now give up further rights without receiving a specific and immediate benefit increase in return, asked representatives of organized labor?

And Democrats demonstrated a willingness to meet Wilson more than half way. Of the 33 amendments the Democrat-controlled Insurance Committee made to Wilson's plan, all but five were acceptable to Assembly Republicans.

In the end, however, there was a certain symmetry to the spectacle, a kind of reassuring familiarity in the way the forces of money and politics played themselves out to exhaustion. Throughout the abbreviated, two-day session, Wilson took every opportunity to highlight his differences with the Democrats and to ignore the remarkably broad areas on which there was agreement. He seemed anxious to continue his attacks on Democrats as he pursues his goal of a Republican majority in the Assembly. The special interests that have fed at the trough of workers' compensation will no doubt return some of their gains to favored candidates during the final days of this bitter political season.

A nd workers, at least those who have had the misfortune to be tossed into the grinding machinery of the workers' compensation system, will remain suspicious and angry at those who seem to fare so much better than they do, for the essence of this debate is a kind of class warfare. Workers mistrust the motives and intentions of their bosses. Employers secretly believe all their workers are out to cheat them. And no system, political or industrial, survives and thrives in such an unhealthy environment. 🏛

THE JUSTICE SYSTEM

California has often been praised for the excellence of its state and local governments— relatively free of scandal, with high-quality civil servants, nationally respected governors (Hiram Johnson and Earl Warren among them) and a Legislature that at least once ranked first in a national survey. But perhaps the state's greatest gift to the nation was the leadership of its Supreme Court. Under a series of forceful chief justices — among them Phil Gibson, Roger Traynor and Donald Wright — the state's highest tribunal often led the way for the United States Supreme Court. The California Supreme Court built a reputation for activism and independence with decisions that struck down the death penalty (People v. Anderson, 1972), outlawed the state's system of financing public education (Serrano v. Priest, 1971) and invalidated an anti-fair housing initiative approved by the electorate (Mulkey v. Reitman, 1966).

The judiciary may be the most powerful of the three branches of state government because the Constitution is so detailed and because the Supreme Court has the power — which it had not been hesitant to use — to strike down acts of the Legislature or initiatives that conflict with the state and federal constitutions. The court also uses its power to void acts of the executive branch that violate either a statute or the constitution.

An activist Supreme Court has often been viewed as a second Legislature — more powerful than the first. Governor Ronald Reagan sought to reduce the activism of the court through his appointments, but one of the big disappointments of his eight years as governor was that his appointee for chief justice, Donald Wright, turned out to be another activist.

In 1977, Democratic Governor Edmund G. Brown Jr. had an opportunity to recast the court and by 1981 his appointees comprised a majority on the court. He appointed the court's first woman, Chief Justice Rose Elizabeth Bird; first black, the late Wiley W. Manuel; and first Latino, Cruz Reynoso. Bird was a highly controversial figure when she was appointed and throughout her tenure on the court. While there were many criticisms of the Bird court by conservatives, the most critical was the court's failure to allow any executions during her tenure as Chief Justice. (Polls indicate that over 80 percent of California citizens favored the death penalty.)

In November 1986, in an unprecedented election, three of the Brown-appointed liberals, Justices Bird, Reynoso and Joseph Grodin lost their confirmation elections. This enabled Governor George Deukmejian to appoint three new conservatives to the high court. These three combined with two previous appointments gave the court a conservative majority which it has retained to date.

Lower and appellate courts

The Supreme Court sits at the apex of the California judicial system. There are three lower levels — the justice and municipal courts, the superior courts, and the district courts of appeal. Members of the Supreme Court and the district courts of appeal are appointed by the governor subject to confirmation by the Commission on Judicial Appointments (consisting of the chief justice, the attorney general and one appeals-court justice). In recent years, the commission has called for public hearings on controversial appointees. Bird was approved by a 2-1 vote following a heated public debate. Incumbent judges' names appear on the ballot at the first general election following their appointment and again at the end of each 12-year term. If the incumbent receives a majority of "yes" votes for retention, he or she has another 12-year term.

• *Municipal and justice courts.* These local courts hear misdemeanor cases, preliminary hearings on some felony charges, small-claims actions and civil cases involving relatively small amounts of money (less than $25,000 in both municipal and justice courts).

• *Superior courts.* These countywide courts hear juvenile criminal cases, felonies, appeals from justice and municipal court decisions, and civil cases that cannot be tried in the municipal courts.

• *Courts of appeal.* These are divided into six districts (based in San Francisco, Los Angeles, Sacramento, San Diego, Fresno, and San Jose). Each division within each court contains three or four justices, with three justices normally sitting on each appeal. The court has jurisdiction over appeals from superior-court actions and decisions of quasi-judicial state boards.

• *The Supreme Court.* The state's highest court handles appeals from the district courts of appeal, although some cases can be taken directly from the trial court to the Supreme Court. In death-penalty cases, for example, appeals automatically go from the superior court to the Supreme Court. The high court also reviews orders of the Public Utilities Commission and has some appointive powers.

Judges of the municipal, justice and superior courts are elected by the people for six-year terms. Vacancies in justice court positions are filled by the county supervisors; the governor fills vacancies in the municipal and superior courts. On occasion, there is a wide-open race for a judgeship, but usually the post is filled by appointment and the incumbent retains the judgeship at the ensuing election.

A judge may be removed or otherwise disciplined by the Supreme Court — but only upon recommendation of the Commission on Judicial Performance, which is composed of five judges, two attorneys and two lay people. Judges are also subject to impeachment and recall, but the more common disciplinary procedure is through an investigation by the commission and action by the high court.

The state Judicial Council is a 21-member board charged with the overall administration of the court system. It is headed by the chief justice, who in turn appoints most of the members. The Administrative Office of the California Courts is the staff agency charged with carrying out the council's policies and conducting research for the council.

California uses the standard jury system. Grand juries (19 citizens in most counties, 23 in Los Angeles) investigate public agencies and have the power to hand down criminal indictments. However, the state Supreme Court ruled in 1978 that preliminary (probable-cause) hearings must be held, whether or not a suspect is indicted. Trial juries usually consist of 12 registered voters, but both sides in a case can agree to a smaller panel or waive a jury and submit the case to a judge. A unanimous vote is needed for acquittal or conviction in a criminal case.

California's Court System

JUDICIAL COUNCIL

Makes rules on judicial procedure; surveys and expedites judicial business.

COMM. ON JUDICIAL PERFORMANCE

Recommends to Supreme Court censure, removal or retirement of judges.

COMM. ON JUDICIAL APPOINTMENTS

Confirms or rejects appointees of Governor to Supreme Court and Courts of Appeal.

U.S. SUPREME COURT

CALIFORNIA SUPREME COURT

Original jurisdiction: writs of mandamus, prohibition, habeas corpus, certiorari.

Appellate jurisdiction: discretionary power to review and decide cases transferred from courts of appeal; appeals from superior court involving death penalty.

DISTRICT COURTS OF APPEAL

1ST DISTRICT	2ND DISTRICT	3RD DISTRICT	4TH DISTRICT	5TH DISTRICT	6TH DISTRICT
San Francisco	Los Angeles	Sacramento	San Bernardino San Diego	Fresno	San Jose

Appellate jurisdiction: appeals from superior courts. Original jurisdiction: habeas corpus, mandamus, certiorari, prohibition.

SUPERIOR COURTS
(one in each county)

Original jurisdiction: Civil-amount in controversy exceeds $15,000, mandamus, habeas corpus, equitable relief, probate, family law and juvenile court matters. Criminal-felonies.

Appellate jurisdiction: appeals from municipal and justice courts.

MUNICIPAL COURTS
(one in each judicial district of more than 40,000)

Civil jurisdiction: amount in controversy, $15,000 or less. Criminal: lesser misdemeanors, preliminary hearings for felonies, infractions.

JUSTICE COURTS
(one in each judicial district of 40,000 or less)

Civil jurisdiction: amount in controversy, $15,000 or less. Criminal: misdemeanors, preliminary hearings for felonies, infractions.

The constitution of the State of California provides that judicial power of the state is vested in a Supreme Court, Courts of Appeal, Superior Courts, Municipal Courts, and Justice Courts (Article VI, section I). Provision is also made for a Judicial Council (Article VI, section 6), a Commission on Judicial Appointments (Article VI, section 7), and a Commission on Judicial Qualifications (Article VI, section 8).

Recommendations, advice, confirmation.

Lines of appeal or review.

The Supreme Court's revolving door

Is all the turnover good for the high Court?

By Robert Egelko

Reprinted from *California Journal*, July 1990

It took an $11 million campaign in 1986 to get Chief Justice Rose Bird and Justices Cruz Reynoso and Joseph Grodin off of the state Supreme Court. Getting their three successors to leave was a lot cheaper: $86,371 a year, apiece — the price of a pension.

Justices John Arguelles, Marcus Kaufman and David Eagleson, the veteran jurists appointed by Governor George Deukmejian when he remade the Court in 1987, announced their retirements with little fanfare or emotion after two, three and four years' service, respectively.

The departures prompted one commentator to talk gloomily of a "turnstile Court." They also were a sign that the death penalty, the

---

Robert Egelko covers the state Supreme Court from the San Francisco bureau of the Associated Press.

downfall of the Bird Court, continues to serve up an intractable problem for the state's judiciary.

Arguelles, 61 when he retired, and Kaufman, 60, later outlined their reasons to reporters — reasons that were predictable. (Eagleson, 65, is keeping mum until he steps down officially next January.) The two had each spent more than two decades on the bench, done their part to get the Court back on its feet, and wanted to spend more time with their families. The workload was rewarding but arduous (Arguelles) or "overwhelmingly tedious" (Kaufman), yet they might have stayed if they hadn't been confident the Court was in good hands, and if they weren't newly eligible for

Bird   **Lucas**

maximum pension benefits.

Speaking separately from one another, Arguelles and Kaufman explained how the judges' pension system discouraged them from remaining on the bench. (Both are now associated with large Southern California law firms, where they no longer work most nights and weekends and presumably make more than the justices' $115,161 annual salary.) They wouldn't have been penalized for staying a little longer — only a judge who remains past 70 suffers a cut in future benefits, from 75 to 50 percent of salary — but once a judge has 20 years on the bench the maximum pension eligibility is reached at age 60. After that, judges must keep contributing 8 percent of their salary to the pension fund.

"It's almost like working for nothing," Arguelles said. Besides, he observed, Deukmejian had been good enough to appoint him, and, "I decided that with the Court stabilized, and with the awareness that [Deukmejian] would name my successor — and I had confidence in his abilities to select a very able person — I felt that I could leave ...The Court has continued to function in my absence."

In other words: no big deal. Judges come and go, but the Court endures — at least the current, stabilized court. Joyce Kennard, 48, has replaced Arguelles, Armand Arabian, 55, has taken Kaufman's spot, and Deukmejian will shortly name another of his appellate justices to succeed Eagleson, who leaves two months after his 20th anniversary on the bench. Only the faces change, getting younger and further from early retirement incentives.

Kaufman even speculated that Deukmejian had deliberately picked three judges who were close to retirement age in 1987, intending them to be "interim appointees."

That was denied by Marvin Baxter, who was Deukmejian's appointments secretary in 1987 and now is a justice on the Fifth District Court of Appeal in Fresno and a candidate to succeed Eagleson. "I don't know of any way anyone can ever predict the tenure of a judge," Baxter said. Kaufman disclaimed any inside knowledge, but his sugges-

tion had a certain plausibility, based on the premise that Deukmejian was familiar with his judges' thinking.

It is perhaps unfair to imply that these are peculiarly the actions of Republican appointees, who think of the Court as a stepping-stone to a comfortable corporate practice. Justices of all political stripes have resigned over the years for reasons both profound and mundane; Justice Otto Kaus, a Jerry Brown appointee, quit in 1985 after four years with much the same explanation as the recent retirees; and Justice Frank Newman, another Brown appointee, left after an even briefer stay in 1982 to return to teaching. It may also be only an historical irony that membership on the Court is treated as relatively inconsequential less than four years after an election in which it was seen as holding the balance of power in California.

The three defeated justices, however, who spent over $2.5 million trying to keep their jobs, could be forgiven for viewing their successors as insufficiently devoted to the Court, although they have not said so publicly. Grodin, now a law professor, refused to criticize the new retirees, commenting only in the abstract that it hurt the Court's reputation and prestige "to regard it as a place where people can come and go casually."

"If someone of the U.S. Supreme Court were to resign because they thought they didn't have anything more to

Grodin   **Reynoso**

gain in pension by staying on and they could make a lot of money by private practice or private judging, I think we would be quite astonished," the former justice said.

This is not the U.S. Supreme Court, of course — there is no life tenure, and the rulings bind no one outside of California — but not long ago it was generally placed in the top rank of the nation's state courts. That image took a battering during the 1986 election. One who saw it as further harmed by the recent retirements was J. Anthony Kline, Governor Jerry Brown's former legal affairs secretary and chief judge-screener and now a Brown-appointed presiding justice on the 1st District Court of Appeal in San Francisco.

"I think what these departures are doing is reinforcing a diminished image of the California Supreme Court and an increasing view that it is not as much the apex of a legal career," Kline said. "The most ominous message ... is that the [state] Supreme Court is no longer seen as the best job that a lawyer or judge could have."

The "turnstile Court" label came from Gerald Uelmen, dean of the Santa Clara University Law School, who has become a kind of unofficial statistician of the Court as well as one of its foremost commentators. One of his studies showed that the average stay on the Court between 1936 and 1986 was 13 years.

"I think the days of long tenure on the Court may well

be over," Uelmen said. Rapid turnover, he said, is "very disruptive," and hurt the Court's "long-term stability and predictability." Grodin had a similar view: Great state courts are usually those whose stable memberships give them "a kind of institutional coherence."

But words like "prestige," "reputation" and "stability" may mean one thing to a law professor or the legal community, and quite another to the general public.

However the Bird Court may have been regarded in academic circles — a matter of considerable debate — it was rejected by the voters after a campaign that subjected the Court to an unprecedented level of public scrutiny. Californians may no longer know who their justices are, but their esteem for, or at least acceptance of, the Court has evidently been restored; all five Deukmejian appointees are to be on the ballot this November, and it would be astonishing if any encountered substantial opposition. As for stability and continuity, as Arguelles noted, one set of Deukmejian appointees has replaced another; the character of the Court — the majority's background and overall outlook, and the kinds of decisions that can be expected — remains the same.

Why, then, should anyone outside of a narrow circle of Court-watchers and appellate lawyers care about the resignations on the state's highest Court?

There are a few reasons.

First, the Court has severely curtailed its role as the arbiter of civil law in California — the area of its work that affects its constituents the most, as homeowners and renters, employers and employees, insurance buyers, injury victims and taxpayers. Turnover is an important contributor to the slowdown, though not the only one.

According to Uelmen's latest study, the Court issued only 105 written decisions in the 12 months ending March 31st — down from a normal pace of 140 the previous year. Just 28 rulings were in civil cases, compared to 43 in routine lawyer discipline cases, with the rest in capital and other criminal cases. The decline was even more drastic in the number of cases accepted for hearing — the Court's mech-

Arguelles

Kaufman

anism for determining its docket: just 80, compared with a 10-year average of 268.

The downturn coincided with the debut of Kennard, who is by all accounts a hard worker and a fast learner. She wrote only two majority opinions during the year. A similar initiation period can be expected for Arabian, appointed this year, and for Eagleson's successor next year.

"It takes at least a year for somebody to break in on the Court, particularly in the death-penalty cases," said Grodin, who served for four years. "A judge who has served on the Court of Appeal [which doesn't handle capital cases] hasn't had any exposure to that stuff. Even after you've broken in,

you don't really hit full stride till you've been there for a few years."

"The justices appear to be working harder than ever, with less to show for it," Uelmen said in his study. (Some

Kennard

Arabian

current and former justices have complained about regularly working six or seven days a week.)

The impact of the drop-off can be striking in individual cases. As the state's high Court accepts fewer cases, the last word on more and more of them belongs to the six appellate courts, each with judges of varying views and abilities and extremely low public profiles. And when a case is accepted for Supreme Court review, it can languish undecided for years.

The most notorious current example is a dispute over the power of the state Fair Employment and Housing Commission to award damages to discrimination victims for emotional distress and other types of harm they suffer, aside from loss of pay. The lawsuit, based on events that took place in 1980-81, was granted a hearing by the Bird Court in 1986 but has never been calendared for oral argument. Meanwhile, the commission has continued to award damages for emotional trauma — the largest single element of many of its cases, such as sexual harassment suits — but the awards are routinely appealed and tied up in lower state courts, which have issued conflicting rulings on their legality. The Legislature has twice passed bills to declare the commission's authority to award limited damages, but Deukmejian has vetoed them, saying the issue was before the Court. No one knows what the law is.

Instead of issuing rulings, the Court has turned to the arcane and much-criticized practice of "depublishing" appellate decisions as its most common method of shaping the law (see "Depublication," *CJ*, April 1985).

Only about 10 percent of Court of Appeal rulings are certified by those courts to be published in books of reported decisions, which can be cited as precedent by other judges and lawyers; once final, they become binding on trial courts statewide. ("Unpublished" appellate rulings are binding only on the parties.) However, the state Supreme Court, when deciding not to accept a case for review, can order a published appellate ruling erased from the books, leaving the result of the case unchanged but destroying its status as precedent. Depublication, unique to California, is supposed to indicate dissatisfaction with some aspect of the lower court's reasoning, but the high Court is not required to state its own reasons and never does. As a result, while it may remove some unwanted language from the casebooks, the process usually leaves everyone in the dark as to the Supreme Court's view of the law.

Abuse of the depublication process was one charge

leveled by prosecutors against the Bird Court, although Bird herself disliked depublication and usually dissented from it. The current Court under Chief Justice Malcolm Lucas is depublishing about 130 cases a year — twice the Bird Court's rate, and last year depublished more cases than it decided.

Depublication casts the Court in the inapt role of censor rather than interpreter of the law and "injects a real

---

UPDATE

Governor Pete Wilson made his first appointment to the state Supreme Court when he named Ronald George, former Associate Justice of the Court of Appeal in Los Angeles. Confirmed in September 1991, George replaced Associate Justice Allen Broussard, who retired.

---

mystery into the law," said Uelmen. But the justices have accepted the practice as a necessary evil to keep their caseload under control, as long as they lack the time to decide all pressing legal disputes themselves.

The chief reason for the lack of time is the death penalty — the grim omnipresence of California law and politics. It undid the Bird Court and has disrupted — perhaps even dominated — the Lucas Court. Bird, Reynoso and Grodin were unseated largely because the Court upheld only four of 68 death sentences — a rate that proved politically unacceptable in a state that had not ousted a Supreme Court justice in 50 years. The current Court has affirmed more than 70 percent of its death sentences and decided the cases three times as fast, solving the political problem but creating a logistical mess.

Lucas, promoted to chief justice by Deukmejian in 1987, faced a backlog of 170 capital cases that had grown to 200 by the time Arguelles, Kaufman and Eagleson completed their shakedown year. He decided to make those cases the Court's top priority; in one dizzying year, the justices produced a record 56 death-penalty rulings but succeeded only in whittling the backlog down to its earlier size. The pace has slowed markedly since then due to turnover, reordering of priorities and the disruption, although about three-fourths of the cases are in early paperwork stages and not yet ready for Court arguments.

Arguelles, who usually voted with the majority to affirm death sentences, recently lent support to suspicions voiced by defense lawyers but denied by prosecutors — that the Lucas Court, by upholding death cases regularly, had encouraged prosecutors around the state to file more death-penalty charges, increasing still further the number of appeals the Court will have to review in the future.

The death cases, which the Court is required by law to review directly from the trial courts, occupy between 25 to 40 percent of the justices' time, by different members' estimates. The trial transcripts run thousands of pages, lawyers are required to raise every conceivable argument, and few important legal issues remain after 12 years of wrestling with the state's last death-penalty initiative.

The capital cases, though, are a response to the public's demand for the death penalty. The public also demanded a stiffening of the State Bar's disciplinary system, and the result has been an upsurge of routine lawyer misconduct cases, which also must be reviewed directly by the Supreme Court, and which occupy an increasing portion of the justices' time. They have far less time than they need to tackle everything else on their plate, including issues of civil law that affect millions of people and offer the kind of intellectual challenge the Court is supposed to provide.

Kaufman said the excessive time spent on death cases was one reason, among many, for his retirement. Arguelles called the cases "cumbersome" but said they didn't hasten his departure. Eagleson, in a speech last year, denied that capital cases or "judge burnout" were serious problems for him or his colleagues. Uelmen said the response sounded like a "party line," and he was not alone in his doubts.

Gideon Kanner, a Loyola University law professor and a conservative counterpart to the liberal Uelmen, pointed critically to the 77 percent of the Court's opinions last year consisting of capital cases, other criminal cases and lawyer discipline.

Calling the Court's turnover alarming but understandable, Kanner wrote in a recent op-ed piece, "Few sensible men and women of great professional achievement are willing to spend the rest of their active lives poring over mountains of verbiage, responding to routine demands of society's dregs."

"It's hard not to conclude that the burden of death-penalty cases is wearing the justices down and burning them out," said Stephen Barnett, a UC Berkeley law professor.

The Court is likely to rid itself soon of automatic review of lawyer misconduct cases. A far more substantial and daring step would be to transfer initial review of capital cases to the Court of Appeal. Supreme Court review would still be required of all affirmed death sentences, but the idea is that appellate courts could weed out some of the flawed cases, distill the factual record and spread the workload around.

The longstanding proposal, which would probably require a state constitutional amendment, was endorsed recently by Arguelles and Kaufman. Bernard Witkin, a prominent California legal commentator, has said it's the only way the Court can get its caseload under control. But the present prospects are doubtful.

For one thing, Lucas said several years ago that the plan would only add another layer of delay; without his support, there would be little chance of legislative approval. Also, most appellate justices are opposed, for good reason: Their job carries the closest thing to guaranteed life tenure of any elected state office — a status that might change quickly for anyone with a record of death-penalty reversals. In fact, even if the transfer took place, it probably would only defer most of the high Court's death-penalty burden temporarily; relief seems possible only by either abolishing capital punishment, eliminating most of the defendants' constitutional safeguards, or adopting Justice Stanley Mosk's equally problematic proposal to split the Court into civil and criminal divisions.

For the moment, the Court's turnstile may slow down. Justice Edward Panelli, who has complained about the workload, isn't eligible for maximum retirement benefits until 1992. Lucas has been the subject of occasional retirement rumors, which he's denied; Mosk and Justice Allen Broussard have also disavowed any plans to leave, although that could change if a Democrat is elected governor.

But the latest defections could be a warning that the Court, which appeared to regain its health after the convulsions of 1986, is still ailing. 🏛

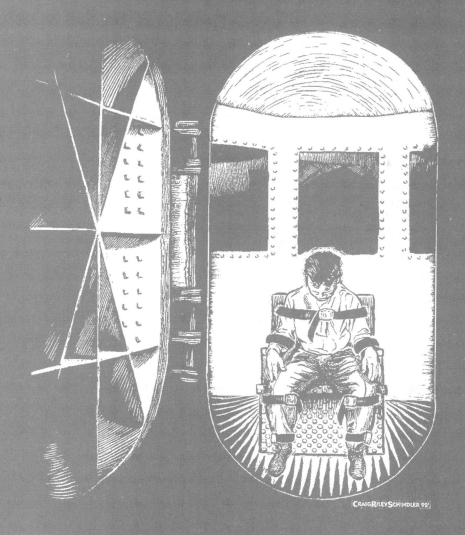

CRAIG RILEY SCHINDLER 92'

The High Cost of Death

By Don Babwin

On Easter morning, April 19th, newspapers all over the country were plastered with headlines about a judge's order to stay the execution of condemned murderer Robert Alton Harris — the first person slated to die in California's gas chamber in 25 years. It was only the latest delay in a case that already had bounced around the courts for nearly 14 years, and angry state officials reacted by saying they would appeal the stay immediately — as in Easter Sunday — to a federal court. And, the stories indicated, the losers in that appeal would take their case to the U.S. Supreme Court the very next day.

Translation: The financial tab on a case that had cost millions of dollars was going to climb at least a little higher, and could have gone a lot higher had the federal high court not put an end to the process. Harris died in San Quentin's gas chamber just after 6 a.m. on Tuesday, April 21st, his last appeal having been emphatically rejected by the Court less than an hour earlier.

To be sure, when talking about the ultimate punishment, there are more important aspects to consider than money. But with more than 300 residents of San Quentin's Death Row all waiting in the wings with their own lengthy and costly appeals, the death penalty represents a major financial strain on an already strapped state budget. Opponents of the death penalty say to execute the prisoners already on death row would cost $1 billion. Ironically, while proponents of the death penalty say much of that money finances unnecessary and frivolous

Reprinted from *California Journal*, June 1992

Don Babwin is a reporter for The Press-Enterprise *of Riverside.*

appeals, opponents argue that recent developments in the appellate process will mean a shortage of cash needed to finance these cases.

Capital cases are rarely quick and never cheap. For example, while Harris' long legal odyssey generated headlines, the longest resident of death row, Andrew Edward Robertson, is still well back in the appellate pipeline — at the point Harris occupied a decade ago. The cases, which are meticulously researched, may take years to prepare. Just getting to trial may take years. Warren James Bland, the suspected murderer of a 7-year-old South Pasadena girl, has been sitting in county jail for more than five years. His trial in Riverside has yet to begin.

The trials themselves are expensive. In Riverside County, for example, police recently arrested William Suff, a man suspected of killing prostitutes and drug users. It is a good bet that the trial will include a parade of experts dealing with everything from DNA (did Suff rape the women?) to child abuse to answer questions about Suff's past. One county official estimated the case may cost as much as $5 million to $10 million. A complicated murder case might include the testimony of psychiatrists, toxicologists and pathologists. If one side calls such a witness, it is a safe bet the other side is going to call its own "expert" to the witness stand. All of these witnesses cost money.

But how much money is not easy to determine. Defense costs, for example, are confidential until a case becomes final — in other words, until the sentence is carried out. Thus, prosecutors have no way to review defense costs for a single resident of Death Row. The only time prosecutors were able to find out defense costs involved an inmate, Joselito Cinco, who hanged himself a few months after being sentenced to death for murdering two San Diego police officers.

Not counting what Cinco's two attorneys charged San Diego County to defend him, the bill was more than a half-million dollars, according to Richard Neely, the San Diego County assistant district attorney who prosecuted the case. Add what the defense attorneys charged, and the cost to defend Cinco easily reached $1 million, Neely said. That figure does not include what the district attorney's office spent to prosecute Cinco. Neely could not estimate how many hours he spent on the case but said for the eight months it took to try the case, prosecuting Cinco was his job.

At the time Cinco killed himself, his case was in the earliest stage of the appellate process. Legal experts say the appeals are much more expensive than the initial trial. In the Harris case, for example, the attorney general's office spent $750,000 and devoted some 6000 attorney hours to the appeals, according to David Puglia, a spokesman for the attorney general's office.

Capital cases can devastate local economies. "We could not fund one at this point," said Don Hemphill, the auditor of Sierra County. "We might have to cut police, very possibly, and other services."

Hemphill said the county had several capital cases in the 1980s and managed to pay for them. He said the state picked up the bulk of the $500,000 to $700,000 it costs to prosecute the cases, with the county's share 10 percent of that. To a county of 3500 permanent residents, $50,000 to $70,000 is a lot of money, he said.

"The only thing that saved us was the economy was well," Hemphill said. Like other counties throughout the

state, the economic picture has changed for the worse in recent years.

Until recently, counties were reimbursed by the state for defense costs other than attorneys' fees, with the cost of experts and tests being paid for through what is called "987.9 funding" from the state. But that source of money is gone.

"As of about a year ago, that fund dried up," said Elisabeth Semel, a San Diego attorney who has handled death penalty cases. "Counties now have to dig into their own pockets."

In Siskiyou County a few years ago, the fund provided a $266,000 reimbursement from the state, according to Dave Elledge, the county's auditor-controller. For a county with a general fund budget of about $23 million, said Elledge, "That's a lot of money."

"I don't know how we would come up with that," Elledge said. As in Sierra County, Elledge said such a case without special funding from the state would likely mean pink slips for some county employees.

As for the state, the death penalty is a financial drain. In 1989 *The Sacramento Bee* reported that the state could save $90 million a year by abolishing the death penalty. Critics such as Semel say there is no reason to believe that figure would not be even greater today. Considering that it costs the state $24,600-a-year to house a prisoner in San Quentin, according to the state's Department of Corrections, a 40-year stay costs $984,000. Pat Clark of the anti-death penalty group, Death Penalty Focus, said studies show a capital case costs anywhere from $1.8 million to $45 million.

But proponents of the death penalty counter that costs are high because convicted death-row inmates file frivolous, repetitious claims in federal court. These, said David Puglia, drive costs up. Besides, said Puglia, the primary goal of the death penalty has never been to save money. "The death penalty is appropriate for the crimes that it was put on the books to cover," he said. "That is the reason for the death penalty."

There is growing concern among defense attorneys that contrary to the popular perception that too much money is spent on death penalty appeals, the opposite is true. Defense attorneys say they are being priced out of the appellate process and can no longer afford to take the cases.

"We're not getting paid," siad Andrea Asaro, a San Francisco attorney who is presently handling two death-penalty appeals.

What is happening, say attorneys, is that the state Supreme Court is refusing to reimburse them for what they say are absolutely necessary expenses. In 1990 the Supreme Court adopted "payment guidelines" outlining how much it would pay for various phases of capital-case appeals. For example, attorneys are paid $75 an hour. While the Court maintains that the rate is the highest in the country, it is still considerably below the $200-$300 hourly rate attorneys charge paying clients. And according to a February 1992 article in *The Sacramento Bee*, an appeal should take between 815 and 1830 hours per case.

The Court also detailed the maximum rates it would allow for investigators, psychiatrists, paralegals and others who might assist in the appeals. Asaro said the rate of $125 an hour for a psychiatrist is unrealistic. "A psychiatrist can bill $300 to

DEATH continued on page 40

Room at the Inn
Prison Population Growth Slows

By John Berthelsen

Reprinted from *California Journal*, June 1992

From the outside, the new California State Prison at Wasco seems to drain light from the landscape. Flat green fields surround its 20-foot unpainted concrete walls, which in turn are encircled by two rows of chain link fencing topped by razor wire.

For Wasco's builders, this is the prison of the future — a $185-million masterwork of efficient incarceration. Inside the bleak, dun-colored facility, jumpsuited correctional officers bearing H&K 94 semi-automatic rifles stand behind computerized consoles in bulletproof second-floor control rooms. The new prison exercises unparalleled control over inmates, reducing escapes and violent incidents against guards and other inmates in California to the lowest rates in 45 years.

Four institutions much like Wasco, each built to hold about 2450 inmates, stand within a 100-mile radius at the southern tip of the San Joaquin Valley. They are called "270 units" because one prison guard, from behind his computer console, has a clear and unobstructed view of 100 cells arrayed in a 270-degree arc around a large central dayroom. Two more prisons are under construction in Southern California, and an additional six have been authorized throughout the state.

But there is a growing question whether these are prisons of the future or relics of an outmoded approach to crime and punishment. That is because California has dramatically slowed the rate at which offenders are going to jail and prison. In June 1991 there were 101,658 inmates housed in California prisons. By March 29, 1992, that figure had grown by fewer than 1000 inmates, to 102,554. After years of double-digit growth rates, California's prison population will have increased less than 1 percent in 1992. Inmate populations are flattening out. And this trend will have a drastic effect on the prison-building program.

This slowdown in growth of the prison population appears to bring to an end an ironic period in American history. While Wall Street was building the bonfire of the vanities at one end of society, authorities at the other were busy sweeping up the social detritus of an increasingly polarized nation — and locking up more men, women and children than at any time in American history. Wasco and its 14 sister prisons built or under construction in California during the decade of the 1980s are the by-product of this era.

By 1991 about 1.1 million Americans were in federal or state prisons or in local jails at a cost of $20 billion a year, according to the Sentencing Project, a Washington, D.C.-based private prison-reform group. With 455 men and women behind bars per 100,000 population, that put the U.S. far ahead of its nearest

---

John Berthelsen is a former Sacramento reporter who now works for the State Legislature.

competitor, South Africa, with a rate of 311 per 100,000. It was even further ahead of the Soviet Union and its infamous gulags.

California's massive prison establishment helped propel the United States to its bleak stature. While the rest of the nation's inmate population was tripling, the state's inmate population quadrupled during the 1980s, to an imprisoned city the size of Berkeley. Some 75,000-odd more offenders are in California's county and city jails, with yet another 8000 in Youth Authority institutions, giving California, with about 11 percent of the nation's population, nearly 17 percent of those in lockup.

California's experience after this feverish decade of prison construction has profound implications for the rest of the United States. California is a trend-setter. And the trend discovered in California? The biggest prison-building program in the history of the world had very little to do with the crime rate. It had a lot to do with politics and a belief that it was possible for California to build its way out of its crime problem. Likewise, today's slowdown in prison building has to do with politics — politics and economic reality. Local and state governments, beset with debt because of the recession and the drying up of federal revenue sharing funds, can no longer afford excessive crime-fighting.

Prior to this spring's Los Angeles riots, knee-jerk crime-busting had begun to slip as an election issue, replaced by concerns over welfare and illegal immigration. The undeserving welfare recipient had replaced 1988 presidential candidate Michael Dukakis' furloughed murderer, Willie Horton, as the bugbear of public political debate. In California, concerns about police protection as a portion of state spending had slipped to eighth place in the public's awareness, according to Mark De Camillo, associate director of the California Poll. Education is first. Prison building has dropped to 13th, with only about a third of Californians saying corrections spending should be increased. Whether the riots alter this equation remains to be seen.

This changing, pre-riots focus has been reflected in prison construction. Today, at Calipatria, in California's southern Imperial Valley, another prison like Wasco stood vacant for months after its completion. It is now being occupied far later than scheduled. A prison at Delano stands temporarily empty. In striking contrast, less than a year ago correctional officials projected that they would have to build 20 to 30 more Wascos before the end of the century in California to house a prison population expected to more than double again by that time.

The fact is that California was sold a bill of goods during the 1980s. If enough new laws were passed, it was reasoned, and enough people were put in prison, the crime rate would drop. California's version of political correctness for the 1970s and 1980s was tough judges, tough laws, and tough punishment exemplified by prison terms with a minimum of rehabilitation programs. To fight what was perceived as a rising crime rate, state and local governments passed hundreds of new laws creating stiff penalties for criminal behavior and drug abuse.

In some ways, the preoccupation with crime was a political perception, fueled in part by a population that was increasing on a steep curve throughout the decade of the 1980s. Although the arrest rate per 100,000 remained relatively stable during the 1980s, the number of those who committed crimes increased. The perception of rampant crime further was aided by highly-publicized crime related to crack cocaine and by drive-by shootings, which acutally added little to the overall crime rate.

"We didn't have to have a crime wave in the 1970s and 1980s," says the staff director of a California-based criminal justice panel. "The public's tolerance for crime decreased. There was a long, continuous period of crime which to the public became intolerable. It became a political issue."

There was no more dramatic example of crime as a political issue than what happened in 1980 to Democratic state Senator Albert Rodda, then 67 and the respected veteran of 22 years in the Legislature. A strong liberal, he had been considered the state's most important influence in public education. But Rodda was unexpectedly unhorsed by a then-29-year-old conservative Republican unknown named John Doolittle. The centerpiece of Doolittle's effort was a $90,000 radio-television campaign that accused Rodda of refusing "to vote on legislation to increase penalties for repeat sex offenders like the East Area Rapist." The so-called East Area Rapist, who was never caught or identified, had been terrorizing a Sacramento neighborhood for months, allegedly committing more than 30 rapes.

The effect of Rodda's defeat on the 120 members of the state Legislature was galvanic. From the date of his loss onward, few lawmakers considered themselves safe without sponsoring a host of anti-crime bills, and voting for hundreds more. Passage of these bills added thousands of inmates to the system, at enormous cost to taxpayers.

Former Governor George Deukmejian was the herald of the state's philosophy of punitive justice. During a long government career, Deukmejian was personally responsible for dozens of crime bills, among them two voter initiatives that alone raised the population of California's prisons by 10,000. Deukmejian fought implacably — and successfully — for restoration of the death penalty after it was voided in 1972 by the courts. In his eight years as governor beginning in 1982, the Legislature sent Deukmejian 350 bills extending or enhancing prison and jail sentences. They encompassed increased penalties for everything from beating an elephant (a misdemeanor sparked by a television report on an animal park) to residential burglary and robbery, manslaughter, murder, certain drug and sex offenses, crimes against defenseless victims, crimes involving the use of a firearm, and many others. Probation was restricted or eliminated for crimes including residential burglary, child molestation, specific sex offenses, arson and other offenses involving the use of firearms.

Deukmejian signed them all.

"I don't think the [legislative] committees are putting out any bills today that aren't necessary," Deukmejian said in a 1991 interview that reviewed his career. "I can't recall any specific ones where I would have said, 'We don't need this.'"

Attempts to rein in this flood of anti-crime legislation have persistently failed in the face of potential voter wrath. A recommendation in a legislative report released in 1991 that all new anti-crime legislation contain a cost appropriation to pay for it has so far been ignored. In the 1991 state legislative session, for instance, 39 new measures extending or enhancing punishments for felonies and misdemeanors were signed into law.

Inevitably, California came to need thousands of new prison beds — at an average cost of $95,000 per two-bed prison cell, although California prison policy, usually violated because of prison overcrowding, is to house one inmate in each cell.

So today, California maintains 23 prisons, 10 reception centers, 41 work camps and 60 community correction facilities. It dwarfs the second-biggest prison system in the U.S., the federal government's own, which is little more than half the size. More than one in six of California's 170,000 state employees is in the Department of Corrections.

According to Deukmejian, it was all necessary. "The fact is that if we didn't have these 100,000 inmates in the state system today, they would be on the streets committing more crimes," he says today. "While the crime rate is still too high, nevertheless it would have been much higher had we not gone forward with a stronger enforcement program and making facilities available for convicted criminals."

But California never did build its way out of its crime problem. There were always more prisoners than prisons. By 1990 prison beds filled every gymnasium in every California prison. In 1991 overcrowding was rated by corrections officials at 186 percent of capacity. It was estimated then that at any given time 5000 inmates — the population of two prisons — were doing what inmates call "road time," being transferred from one institution to another.

What effect did this massive lockup have on crime? In contrast to these skyrocketing prison population rates, nothing appears to have changed much in the crime rate per 100,000 of population.

Most crime is committed by those under 29 years of age, particularly males who are poor and uneducated. When the huge mass of baby boomers born between 1945 and 1955 began to age, crime dropped markedly. Most crime peaked in 1980 (at about 3905 reported crimes per 100,000 of population) and began a steady downward trend. By 1985 the index of major crimes — murder, robbery, assault, forcible rape, burglary and vehicle theft — dropped to 3142, then began rising slightly in the mid-1980s. By 1990 reports of violent crime had risen to about 3394 per 100,000, although a significant part of that increase was due to the reclassification of domestic violence as aggravated assault, a violent crime.

In fact, arrest rates are likely to surge and decline for manifold reasons that have nothing to do with the laws that are passed. They include the political agendas not only of the Legislature and local governments but of the 490 police chiefs, 58 county sheriffs and 58 district attorneys in California. They also depend to a great extent on discretion — first, for instance, on whether the aggrieved citizen reports the crime. In large numbers of felonies, no complaint is filed. The mugged commuter, the raped date, the driver whose car stereo is stolen, grimly forgets it because he or she doesn't believe the police can or will do anything.

Next, there is the discretion and aggressiveness of the arresting officer, and after that, the discretion of the prosecutor in filing charges, the discretion of the jury, and finally the discretion of the judge in sentencing.

Thus, as accused felons funnel into the system, they drop out in dramatic numbers. California local jurisdictions reported one million felony complaints in 1990. Arrests were made in 577,000 cases. Prosecutors filed charges in 209,000.

Of those adjudicated, 169,000 individuals were found guilty and 53,342 were sent to prison.

Now, like the prison incarceration rate, the arrest rate has begun to do funny things that demonstrate how economic or political concerns come into play. The arrest rate began falling in early 1991, at least partly because of an arcane change in the state budget passed in July 1990. California's counties, faced with declining revenues, had asked the Legislature for some relief for their fiscal pain. State lawmakers allowed counties to garner some revenue by collecting fees from cities for each arrestee booked into county jails — the entry point for the vast majority of law violators into the criminal-justice system.

The law went into effect on January 1, 1991, and the consequences were dramatic. According to raw data supplied by the state's Bureau of Criminal Statistics, total arrests for the first six months of 1991 fell by nearly 10 percent over the previous year as cities, faced with stretching their own budgets to pay rent for their prisoners in county jails, cut back on aggressive policing.

Many criminologists also are convinced that at least part of the current dip in arrest rates in California, and particularly Los Angeles, occurred because of the shocking videotaped beating of motorist Rodney King by Los Angeles police officers in March 1991. The videotape was widely shown nationwide and caused police to be more cautious in arrests, the criminologists say.

Another reason for the decline in arrests was particularly noticeable in drug and narcotics apprehensions. In the first six months of 1990, 75,968 offenders were arrested for narcotics-related offenses. But in the first six months of the following year, that had fallen to 61,947 — a decrease of 18 percent. This is because, across the state — and the nation — law enforcement agencies, responding to changing neighborhood politics and strapped by diminishing resources, no longer had the money or personnel for wide-ranging sweeps that dragged in low-level drug traffickers and users.

"Law enforcement agencies respond in various ways to communities," says Cary Rudman, a criminal-justice specialist with the California Legislature. "Today many of them, particularly [in] middle-class communities where drugs and many drug-related crimes have now abated, are more concerned about traditional personal and property crime."

Consequently, Rudman continues, "Law enforcement has responded with the newest hot button term in the law-enforcement lexicon — neighborhood policing, which used to be called beat patrols." That, Rudman says, takes away resources from inner cities where drug trafficking, use and drug-related crime takes place. Drug trafficking is continuing unabated in these areas. "The police have just chosen to redirect most of their efforts elsewhere. We just declared victory and got out."

Another reason for California's sudden static prison population came with the new gubernatorial administration in Sacramento. Crime-fighter George Deukmejian was replaced by Pete Wilson, who considers himself a manager of bureaucracies. Not that Wilson wants to project a soft-on-crime image. Faced with a massive fiscal crisis that amounted to nearly $15 billion in 1991 and may hit $12 billion for the fiscal year that ends June 30, 1992, Mr. Wilson is nonetheless embracing tough crime bills that would keep rapists behind bars for at least 18 years and lock up child molesters for life.

Such Wilson-sponsored legislation could add 12,000 prisoners to the system, cost $250 million a year and another $500 million in capital costs for new prisons. Yet another Wilson-sponsored measure would eliminate credit for work in prison against time served, which could cost as much as $1 billion more a year because of the additional time inmates would have to serve, according to state budget analysts.

However, shortly after he took office in January 1991, Wilson appointed as his prisons and paroles czar former deputy corrections director James Gomez, a career bureaucrat who previously served as deputy director of the Social Services Department. While Wilson preached a hard-line message at one end of the system, Gomez flew around the state, reining in overachieving parole officers who were sending great numbers of their charges back to prison for minor violations. The number of parolees on the street has jumped by 14.5 percent.

At the start of the Deukmejian administration in 1983, 27 percent of male felon parolees were returned to prison for various violations. That soared to 67 percent by the time Deukmejian left office. By 1990 California was returning almost as many parolees to its prisons as the other 49 states combined. Today, recidivism has fallen to 44 percent, according to Gomez, who adds that he would prefer to have parolees on the street, seeking jobs. The room-and-board cost of housing an inmate in California averages $24,800 in yearly operating funds — nearly $70 a day each.

Accordingly, Gomez has added state employment specialists to 69 parole offices throughout the state. Residential multi-service centers for homeless parolees are also being established.

"Jobs and housing are two of the keys," Gomez says. "I have an opinion that if you don't get a job in 60 days after parole, you are ours. If you don't have a place to live, it is not going to be very long before you are back in the prison system."

So there is little evidence that the hefty prison sentences and tough parole policy cut the crime rate, that these hundreds of new laws and $2.9 billion in new prisons spent so far have bought anything. Will the crime rate go up? Probably, according to a 1991 study the state's Bureau of Criminal Statistics, although what happens to the crime rate will have precious little to do with criminal justice.

"California, unlike most of the nation, has experienced greater immigration and in-migration of young people. Therefore, California's crime trends of the 1990s will most likely be similar to the late 1970s when the age composition was younger," the 1991 study says.

Thus, the crime statistics agency says its most reliable predictive model forecasts an increase in crime over the next 20 years "due to interactions of demographic factors, increasing economic polarization, and drug use among the underclass and youth populations."

Nowhere among these reasons for increasing or decreasing crimes does the Bureau of Criminal Statistics cite tougher judges, stiffer laws, longer prison sentences or better prisons. 🏛

DEATH continued from page 36

$350 an hour," she said. That leaves attorneys in the position of having to pay the fees out of their own pockets.

"You're finding lawyers personally in debt, or refusing to take the cases," said Semel. Asaro said she has spent "thousands of dollars" of her own money on death-penalty cases. Her law partner, Sanford Rosen, was told that a $12,297 bill he submitted for paralegal services was disallowed under the guidelines, according to the *Bee*. Financially, no law firm can handle more than two death penalty appeals, said Asaro. Within the guidelines the Court says it "will provide reasons in writing for fee disallowances of $1000 or more, and expense disallowances of $500 or more."

But, Asaro said, "The reality is they don't need a reason. The only explanation is that [the request for reimbursement] exceeds the guidelines."

Court spokeswoman Lynn Holton said the guidelines were adopted after "extensive Court review and comment from the State Bar, local bars, defense attorneys and the California Appellate Project." Further, she said in a prepared statement read by another Court official, "The Supreme Court follows a careful review process when it evaluates expense claims of court-appointed counsel in capital appeals. Each claim is thoroughly reviewed and nothing is done arbitrarily."

Another development that has defense attorneys worried is the decision by the state Supreme Court to take from the California Appellate Project (CAP) the job of recruiting attorneys to handle the appeals in death-penalty cases. CAP, which had done the recruiting and screening of attorneys, now serves solely as an adviser to the court. The Court said it made its decision because of the growing number of condemned prisoners who were without attorneys. According to an article in the March 25th edition of the legal newspaper, the *Daily Journal*, Associate Justice Ronald George said the Court had to step in because CAP has been "unsuccessful in bringing down the backlog." Since January 1991, George said, the number of condemned prisoners has increased by about 60.

Defense attorneys fear the result will be less-qualified attorneys assigned to death-penalty cases. And George told the *Daily Journal*, "It's our firm intention and desire not to lower the standards."

But attorneys say that has already happened. "The first person they picked was somebody without any complex criminal litigation or appellate experience," said John Cotsirillos, a San Diego attorney who is handling the appeal of convicted murderer Jackson Daniels of Riverside.

The Court's first selection was former Chief Deputy State Public Defender Matthew Newman. According to the *Daily Journal*, Newman "lacks experience in either death penalty or homicide cases..."

Cotsirillos said the guidelines are geared toward experienced attorneys, not attorneys who have never handled complicated appeals. Thus, it is more likely that guidelines might be exceeded, some critics say.

The cost of bringing a convicted felon from crime scene to gas chamber is but one aspect in the growing debate over use of the death penalty. Polls continue to show that a majority of Californians support the death penalty, and reminders about the ultimate cost of such cases are not likely to erode much of that support. But those reminders are instructive, for they show that the price of the ultimate penalty remains high. 🏛

THE LEGISLATURE

California's Legislature is not much different from Congress and legislative bodies in other states in overall power and structure. It is, simply stated, the policy-making arm of government, restricted only by the federal and state constitutions and the governor's veto. Like Congress, it can also conduct investigations into almost any issue of public concern and impeach public officials. The Senate must ratify top-level, non-judicial appointments of the governor, while both houses have the opportunity to reject the executive's nominations for any vacancy among the state's constitiutional offices. It also can ratify amendments to the United States Constitution. In recent years, there has been a trend toward the Legislature's appropriating for itself some of the appointive power traditionally given to the executive. Thus, it is not uncommon now to have a commission consist of both gubernatorial and legislative appointees.

Seats in both the 40-member Senate and 80-member Assembly are apportioned on the basis of population. (Until 1966, the Senate was apportioned by geography, like the United States Senate.) Assembly members serve two-year terms; Senate terms are for four years, with half the terms expiring every two years. Under the provisions of Prop. 140 of November 1990, term limits are now imposed on state legislators (3 terms, 6 years in the Assembly; 2 terms, 8 years in the Senate). The Senate and Assembly are organized differently, with power diffused in a committee of the upper house but centered in the office of speaker in the Assembly.

The Senate

The lieutenant governor is the president of the Senate, but this official has virtually no power. The lieutenant governor is entitled to cast a vote to break a 20-20 tie, but this situation almost never develops. If the Senate can be said to have a single leader it is the president pro tempore, who is elected by a simple majority of his colleagues. The pro tem is charged with overall administration of the house, but the real power — committee appointments and assignment of bills to committee — rests with the five-member Rules Committee. The president pro tempore is chairman, and the other four seats are traditionally divided between the two major parties. Between 1969 and 1975, there was an almost-constant battle for the leadership post between two factions sometimes referred to as the Old Guard and the Young Turks. However, in recent years the divisions in the Senate have tended to be along party lines. There has been stability in leadership, at least among Democrats, since 1980 when David Roberti became president pro tempore.

Aside from the Rules Committee, the two most important panels in the Senate are the Appropriations and Budget and Fiscal Review committees. The Budget and Fiscal Review Committee handles the budget. The Appropriations Committee hears any other bills with direct or implied state cost. Thus it can kill almost any major bill.

The Assembly

The Assembly has a form of government that might be called self-inflicted dictatorship. The speaker is elected by at least 41 votes (a simple majority) and thereafter wields tremendous power; this officer appoints all committee chairs and names all committee members except for the Rules Committee. Control over committees amounts to the power to kill any bill. A bill defeated in committee can be brought to the floor by a majority vote of the full assembly, but this occurs very infrequently. A vote to withdraw a bill from committee would be tantamount to a vote of no-confidence for the speaker. The speaker's control over legislation makes whoever holds this office the second-most-powerful official in state government next to the governor. However, on occasion, the speaker has had difficulty leading. Battles within majority Democratic ranks in 1979-80 between then-Speaker Leo McCarthy and challenger Howard Berman, each with his own faction, led to legislative paralysis in the lower house. In 1988 the "Gang of Five" (anti-leadership Democrats) openly feuded with Democratic Speaker Willie Brown over legislative matters in the Assembly. Though the five were punished by Speaker Brown (losing chairmanships, committee assignments, staff and office space) they refused to back down. For a time, the "Five" combined with the Republican caucus had a majority in the Assembly. However after the November 1988 elections, Democrats had 42 seats plus the rebellious "Gang of Five" who were no longer needed for a majority. The "Five" returned to the Democratic fold, and their transgressions forgiven.

The Rules Committee in the Assembly is primarily a housekeeping group, assigning bills to committees, setting salaries for legislative employees, purchasing supplies, and handling routine resolutions.

Speakers come to power in two ways — by the members of the majority party or by coalition. Speaker Willie Brown formed a coalition with members of both parties in 1981.

In the Assembly the key committee is the Ways and Means Committee. It is the general clearing house for most bills before they reach the floor. This is because no measure with fiscal implications — most important bills — can go from a so-called policy committee directly to the floor.

Both houses have become more partisan in recent years. The Senate only a few decades ago paid little attention to party conflict, but the caucuses have become stronger and it is not unusual now to see party-line votes. Partisanship increased in the Assembly during the Reagan, Deukmejian and Wilson governorships. Further fomenting partisanship, party caucuses are active in campaigns for legislative seats, and their staffs are always at work digging up issues that could prove embarrassing to the opposition.

Legislation

There are three basic types of legislation: bills, constitutional amendments and resolutions. These measures can only be introduced by legislators. The governor cannot introduce a bill, but he can ask a friendly member to put it in the hopper. Even the governor's budget carries the name of a lawmaker. In fact, however, very few bills are the direct inspiration of a legislator. Most bills come from interest groups, staff members, constituents, government officials, or a variety of other sources.

A bill is simply a proposed statute. It can be enacted by a simple majority vote in both houses unless it is an urgency measure or carries an appropriation, in which case a two-thirds vote of approval is required. Constitutional amendments are proposed changes to the state Constitution; a two-

CALIFORNIA'S LEGISLATIVE PROCESS

Initial steps by author

IDEA

Sources of bills: legislators, legislative committees, governor, state and local governmental agencies, business firms, lobbyists, citizens.

DRAFTING

Formal copy of bill and "layman's digest" prepared by Legislative Counsel.

INTRODUCTION

Bill submitted by senator or Assembly member. Numbered and read for first time. Assigned to committee by Assembly or Senate Rules Committee. Printed.

Action in house of origin

COMMITTEE

Testimony taken from author, proponents and opponents. Typical actions: Do pass; amend and do pass; no action; hold in committee (kill); amend and re-refer to same committee; refer to another committee; send to interim study.

Bills with any fiscal implications, if approved by policy committee, are referred to Appropriations Committee in the Senate and to Ways and Means Committee in the Assembly.

SECOND READING

Bills given do-pass recommendations are read a second time and placed on file for debate on a subsequent day.

FLOOR DEBATE AND VOTE

Bills are read a third time and debated. A roll-call vote follows. For ordinary bills, 21 votes are needed in the Senate and 41 in the Assembly. For urgency bills and most appropriations measures, 27 and 54 votes are required. If these numbers are not reached, the bill is defeated. Any member may seek reconsideration and a second vote. If passed or passed with amendments, the bill is sent to the second house.

Disposition in second house

READING

Bill is read for the first time and referred to committee by the Assembly or Senate Rules Committee.

COMMITTEE

Procedures and possible actions are identical to those in the first house.

SECOND READING

If cleared by committee, the bill is read a second time and placed on the daily file (agenda) for debate and vote.

FLOOR DEBATE AND VOTE

The procedure is identical to the first house. If a bill is passed without having been amended in the second house, it is sent to the governor's desk. (Resolutions are sent to the secretary of state's office.) If amended in the second house and passed, the measure returns to the house of origin for consideration of amendments.

Resolution of two-house differences (if necessary)

CONCURRENCE

The house of origin decides whether to accept the second-house amendments. If the amendments are approved, the bill is sent to the governor. If the amendments are rejected, the bill is placed in the hands of a two-house conference committee composed of three senators and three Assembly members.

CONFERENCE

If the conferees fail to agree, the bill dies. If the conferees present a recommendation for compromise (conference report), both houses vote on the report. If the report is adopted by both, the bill goes to the governor. If either house rejects the report, a second (and even a third) conference committee may be formed.

Role of the governor

SIGN OR VETO?

Within 12 days after receiving a bill, the governor may sign it into law, allow it to become law without his signature or veto it. A vetoed bill returns to the house of origin for possible vote on overriding the veto. It requires a two-thirds majority of both houses to override.

Urgency measures become effective immediately after signing. Others usually take effect the following January 1st.

thirds vote of each house will place one of these measures on the ballot for voter consideration. Resolutions are merely statements of legislative viewpoint. They may be addressed to other governmental agencies, describe state general policy, or commend or memorialize someone. They are normally passed by voice vote. Constitutional amendments and resolutions, unlike bills, are not subject to gubernatorial veto.

Legislative process

When a member introduces a bill, its title is read and it is printed. Then it is assigned to a committee by the Assembly or Senate Rules Committee. The committee hearing is the most crucial stage in the legislative process, for it is at this point — not on the floor — that the fate of most legislation is determined. Following public hearing, the committee can kill the measure or send it to another committee (usually the fiscal committee) or to the floor as is or with recommended amendments. When it reaches the floor, the bill's title is read a second time, amendments are often made, and the legislation is placed on the agenda for debate. After debate, a roll call is taken. If the bill is passed, it is sent to the other house, where the same process takes place. If the bill is amended in the second house, it must return to the house of origin for acceptance or rejection of the amendments. If approved at this point, the bill goes to the governor for signature or veto. If the amendments are rejected, a conference committee of three members of each house is formed to compromise differences. This procedure is always followed on the budget and often used at the end of a session to speed the last-minute rush of bills (because a conference committee report can be produced more rapidly than a revised printed version of a bill).

A bill goes to the governor if both houses approve a conference committee recommendation.

In the Senate, roll calls are taken orally by the secretary of the Senate and aides. Once a roll call is concluded, members may not change their votes, and absent members cannot add their votes. The Assembly uses an electronic vote counter. Members push switches, and lights shine on a board — green reflecting aye; red, no. With the unanimous consent of the membership, members are allowed to change their votes the same day or add their votes if their actions do not alter the outcome.

Legislative modernization

Until 1966, the Legislature met for general sessions in odd-numbered years and for short budget sessions in even-numbered years. Legislators then received $6,000 a year, and their elective positions were not considered to be full-time occupations. In 1966, the voters approved Proposition 1a making each year's session unlimited, raising the pay to $16,000 and allowing lawmakers to give themselves cost-of-living increases of five percent a year. In the June 1990 primary election voters approved Prop. 112. While some of the provisions of this constitutional amendment established new ethics regulations, perhaps its key feature was the creation of a new Citizens' Compensation Commission. The reason this amendment was proposed was because the Legislature angered many votes when they voted to increase their salaries. To deflect this criticism the commission was established. In December 1991 the new commission raised salaries of state legislators from $40,816 a year to $52,500. In

addition, legislative leaders received extra compensation: floor leaders, $57,750 each; and the Speaker and Senate President Pro Tem, each receive $63,000.

In 1972, the people approved another constitutional amendment. This one put the Legislature on the same two-year schedule as Congress, with bills remaining alive for two years. The Legislature now is in session year-round, with breaks for Easter, Christmas, part of the summer and during statewide elections. In addition to their salaries, legislators receive $100 a day for expenses and have use of leased automobiles, credit cards and district offices.

In addition to the standing committees, which consider the merits of bills, the Legislature also establishes two-house joint committees and one-house select committees to study specific problems (often of special concern to only one legislator, who becomes chairman of the committee). These committees can submit recommendations to the Legislature but have no direct power over legislation. Many of these select committees have been eliminated under the new budget strictures of Proposition 140.

Legislative staff

Each member of the Legislature has a personal staff plus the assistance of specialists assigned to committees and to the party caucuses. There are also three major independent bureaus with significant influence on the legislative process— the legislative counsel, the legislative analyst, and the auditor general, although the survival of the two latter offices is threatened by budget reductions mandated by Proposition 140.

• *Legislative counsel*, Bion Gregory, has a large staff of attorneys to provide legal advice to lawmakers and draft their bills and proposed amendments.

• *Legislative analyst*, Elizabeth Hill, provides advice to the Legislature on anything with a fiscal implication, which can cover virtually every major bill. The analyst annually publishes a detailed analysis of the governor's budget, which becomes the basis for legislative hearings on the fiscal program.

• *Auditor general*, Kurt R. Sjoberg (acting), conducts investigations of state agencies to determine whether they can be run more economically and efficiently, he reports directly to the Joint Audit Committee and to the Legislature as a whole.

In all, a staff of some 2,000 served the Legislature until the passage of Prop. 140 in November 1990 which mandated term limits for members and budget reductions for the Legislature. The Legislature's staff has been reduced to comply with the measure. In addition to the analyst, auditor general, and counsel, there are sergeants-at-arms, secretaries, political aides, and committee consultants. The consultants are the most important element of the staff; they provide specialized knowledge for committees, gather information and provide independent evaluation of information obtained from interest groups, the governor and others.

Reapportionment

Almost nothing stirs the juices of a legislator — either at the state or federal level — as much as the prospect of his or her district being reapportioned. Whether as a result of court order or the federal census, redistricting has the potential of throwing many legislators out of office. The census is conducted every 10 years at the beginning of a new decade, and every congressional, Senate and Assembly district in California must be redrawn after each census to eliminate population differences.

California's Assembly districts have always been apportioned by population, but the state Senate has been apportioned under two systems. Prior to 1926, the Senate was also apportioned by population, but in that year the voters approved a "federal plan" devised by Northern Californians to keep control of the Senate from rapidly growing Southern California. This plan provided that no county could have more than one senator and that one senator could represent no more than three counties. As a result, the senator from Los Angeles at one time represented 440 times more people than the senator from Alpine, Inyo and Mono counties. This was the most severe apportionment imbalance in the nation. Such discrepancies were eradicated in 1966, when the U.S. Supreme Court's "one-man, one-vote" edict went into effect.

Redistricting is usually fairly simple if both houses of a legislature and the governor are of the same political party. The party in power merely divides the state to suit itself and gives the opposition party the scraps. The usual procedure is to offer some members of the opposition good deals so that a nominally bipartisan reapportionment bill can be passed. Actually, it is impossible to create good districts for one party without fashioning some just as good for the other. But the legislators doing the redistricting can usually pick and choose whom to favor among members of the opposition. In the 1980s reapportionment, although Democrat Jerry Brown was governor and Democrats had solid majorities in both houses, Republicans stymied the majority party's reapportionment plans by qualifying three separate referenda for

the June 1982 ballot. Voters voted "no" against the three Democratic sponsored bills and forced the Democrats to make some adjustments to the district lines.

Under the state Constitution, the Legislature is empowered to reapportion all seats (52 in Congress, 40 Senate and 80 Assembly districts), subject only to a gubernatorial veto. Thus, when a governor is of a different party than the Legislature's leadership an impasse is apt to develop. In this case, either a bi-partisan plan is drawn favoring the incumbents of both parties, maintaining the status quo, or the matter ends up in the courts.

Republicans tried repeatedly in the 1980s to modify the reapportioning process. Their objective was to shift the decision making away from Democratic legislative leaders:

1) In 1982 Republicans joined with Common Cause and qualified Prop. 14 to establish an independent districting commission to do the reapportioning. Voters defeated the proposal.

2) In 1983 then Assemblyman Don Sebastiani qualified a new initiative which provided, he claimed, "fairer" districts than the one the Democrats had devised. This initiative was declared unconstitutional by the state Supreme Court prior to its being voted upon. The court ruled that reapportioning could take place only once each decade.

3) In 1984 Governor Deukmejian authored an initiative to have reapportioning handled by a panel of retired appellate judges. Voters rejected this proposal.

The 1991 reapportionment plans passed by the Democratic-controlled Legislature were vetoed by Republican Governor Pete Wilson. Because of the impasse, districts were drawn by the state Supreme Court with the help of "special masters." Surprisingly, Democrats fared well in 1992 in Assembly, Senate and congressional elections— even with the court-designed districts. 🏛

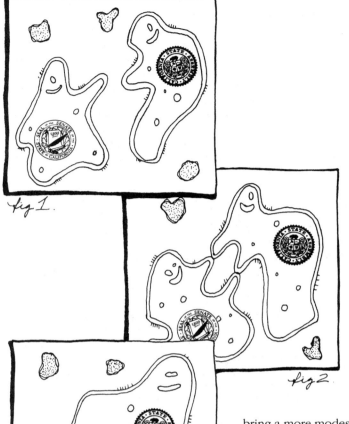

fig 1.

fig 2

fig 3.

PLJ

The unicameral legislature

New look at an old idea

By Jim Richardson

Reprinted from *California Journal*, May 1991

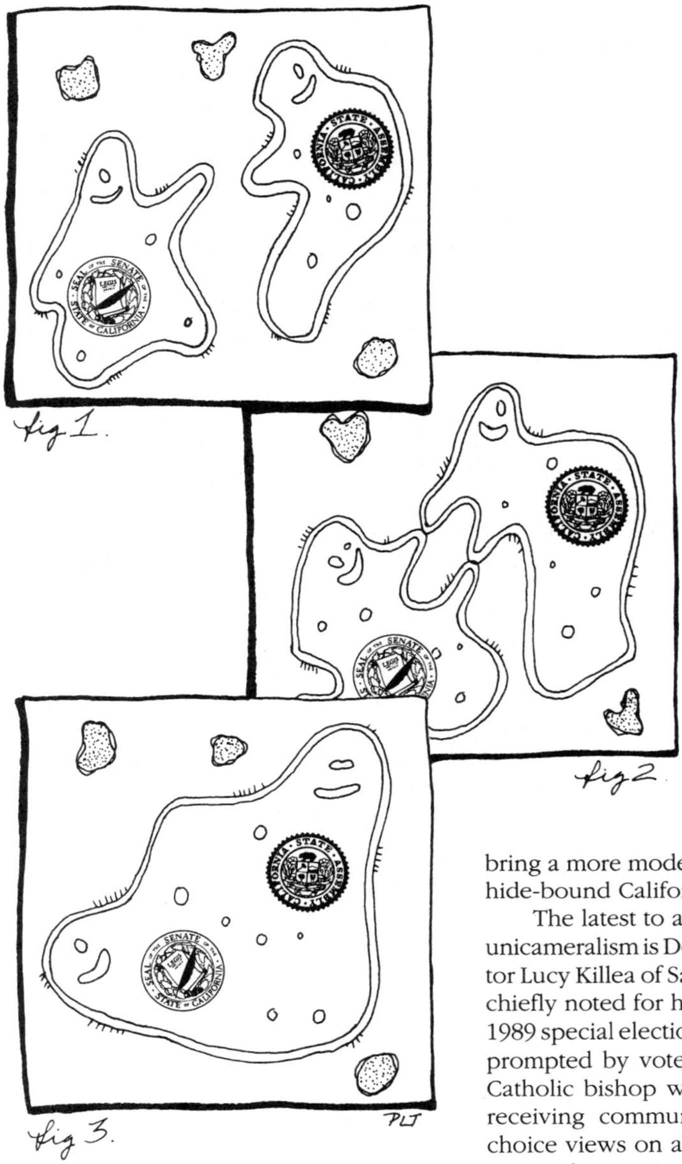

A unicameral legislature in California is an idea whose time probably has not come. But amid the ruin that is the California Legislature in the early going of the 1991-1992 session, that age-old idea has surfaced yet again — and not just among the political scientists who find the subject sport, but among the more cynical breed of lawmakers as well.

The outcome of their dialogue likely will not be a one-house Legislature in the foreseeable future, even its more candid proponents admit. But the discussion, some lawmakers believe, could

Jim Richardson is a reporter in The Sacramento Bee *Capitol bureau.*

bring a more modest *perestroika* to the hide-bound California Legislature.

The latest to advance the cause of unicameralism is Democratic state Senator Lucy Killea of San Diego, heretofore chiefly noted for her upset victory in a 1989 special election — an event in part prompted by voter reaction against a Catholic bishop who barred her from receiving communion over her pro-choice views on abortion.

In the spring of 1991, already frustrated in her new job, Killea busily stumped service clubs and lined up political scientists behind unicameralism. Killea proposes establishing a state constitutional revision commission to work out the details. She took a well-publicized trip to Nebraska, the only state with a unicameral legislature. Killea got a fair amount of news coverage on the issue, particularly in her hometown newspapers (where, perhaps not coincidentally, she has been floating the idea of running for mayor later this year).

"We have certainly ended up with gridlock rather than checks-and-balances," said Killea.

But the last thing some of the Legislature's weary leaders want to think

about is a major reform of their institution at a time when they are grappling with a $12 billion budget deficit and have district reapportionment looming just around the corner. Nor have legislative leaders recovered from the legal confusion of Proposition 73's campaign contribution limits, overturned after a long legal wrangle. They are still trying to get used to Proposition 112, a measure they successfully put forward — with varying degrees of enthusiasm — that drastically restricts gifts and bans honoraria for speeches. And legislative leaders are still in deep shock over term limits and accompanying severe budget cutting required by Proposition 140, approved by voters in November 1990.

"The Legislature can only take so much major restructuring," lamented Democratic Senate President pro Tempore David Roberti of Los Angeles, in an interview on Killea's unicameral proposal. "If every time you turn around there is another proposal to restructure the Legislature, quite frankly we'll never get anything done. At some time we have to concentrate on substantive issues."

Killea's argument is that the Legislature has not focused on substantive issues partly because the two houses are so different. Among the contributing factors to the paralyzing budget impasse of 1990, when the Legislature left the state without authority to spend money for nearly a month, was that the two houses could not reach agreement. Each house became consumed in its own politics. At one point, the Senate passed a budget and left town, leaving a fuming Assembly. One Assembly member had choice words for the Senate's action, calling it "dog doo" left on the front porch.

The idea of a unicameral legislature has a certain appeal — doing away with duplicative legislative functions, consolidating dual committees, bringing forth a degree of efficiency and accountability — to lawmaking. Killea maintains that the only thing stopping a unicameral legislature are "artificial reasons" for having two houses and institutional resistance to change.

"I think the sense of crisis around here is causing people to look at it more closely," said Killea. "What we have isn't working. There are a tremendous number of major issues we haven't been able to deal with even in a minor way."

She got a boost to the cause from no less than Republican John Larson on his way out the door as chairman of the state Fair Political Practices Commission. "You can hide too many things with the two houses here," he said in a newspaper interview endorsing unicameralism. "One house will give you anything you want, knowing the other is going to throw it right in the river."

Killea is not the first to push the unicameral idea. Between 1913 and 1937 there were no fewer than 15 proposed constitutional amendments on the subject put forward by California legislators. The idea was revived in the 1970s by the most successful legislator of the modern era — the late Assembly Speaker Jesse Unruh. But 11 such proposed amendments got nowhere.

"The present two-house system is a costly and inefficient anachronism that thwarts the popular will, caters to private interests and hobbles responsible and responsive decision-making," Unruh said in a widely quoted speech. "Unless unicameralism is made central to the present efforts to reform and modernize state legislatures, I do not believe that increased salaries, new facilities, and professional staff will be more than temporary pal-liatives for the ills that it is hoped they will cure. These reforms in themselves only make a more efficient horse and buggy. I take little comfort from the fact that legislatures can be the fastest horse and buggy in the jet age."

Picking up the mantle, Democratic Assemblyman Tom Bane of Tarzana, now the powerful chairman of the Assembly Rules Committee, tried pushing a unicameral legislature in 1975. His bill was approved by a committee dominated by rebels to then Speaker Leo McCarthy. But it went no further. "Some of the people voted for it just because they wanted to have fun," Bane recently recalled.

The current majority and minority leaders of the state Senate, Democrat Barry Keene of Benicia and Republican Kenneth Maddy of Fresno also pushed unicameral bills in the 1970s and early '80s. Keene and Maddy have signed on as co-authors to Killea's bill.

"There's no reason to have two houses," said Maddy, adding he sees "no chance" for Killea's bill (a reality making it easier to support).

In advancing her bill, Killea took a different approach than in earlier efforts. She proposes increasing the size of the Legislature — although she has not suggested exactly to what size. In effect, Killea proposes giving legislators smaller districts, an idea attractive to many who are otherwise loath to a single-house legislature.

Smaller districts are harder to gerrymander. The cost of getting elected theoretically would be less and serving a smaller number of constituents would be easier. Also, the argument goes, with so many more representatives in the Legislature, it would be harder for a narrow special interest to buy or influence enough votes to dominate an issue.

"There is some logic to that," said Senator William Leonard of Red-lands, the second ranking Republican. Although he calls unicameral-ism a "stupid idea," Leonard likes the idea of a bigger Legislature with smaller districts. However, he points out, smaller districts could be achieved without a single-house legislature. Leonard suggested increasing the size of the Assembly by a three- or four-to-one ratio with the Senate instead of the current two-to-one ratio.

Leonard said that despite predictions to the contrary, the Assembly and Senate have each maintained a distinctive character even after court decisions put Senate districts on the same one-person, one-vote basis as Assembly districts. "Here, theoretically, we should all be duplicates of each other. We're not. And I think that's healthy. That means each of us is looking through different eyes at these same bills to see if they read the same way to each of us."

Maddy, however, said that in reality, the Legislature has killed few bills. Roughly 5000 bills per session landed on then-Governor George Deukmejian's desk and there is no sign the number will be appreciably smaller for Governor Pete Wilson. "There is really not a 'check-and-balance' between the two houses," said Maddy. "The trial lawyers are just as strong over there as they are here. They're not checked-and-balanced."

Lawmakers maintain publicly that they have an open mind toward Killea's proposal. However, many say privately — and a few will say publicly — that the real value to her proposal is in spurring a discussion of the Legislature's unwieldy rules.

Roberti and many Democrats have long argued that the single largest impediment to lawmaking is not the dual-house system but the rule that the state budget must be approved by a two-thirds vote in each house. The rule has allowed a small minority of Republicans — sometimes only in one house — to thwart the will of the majority.

The two-thirds vote rule, however, has been next to godliness and the line-item veto in sanctity with Republicans, who have been in the minority in both houses of the Legislature for 20 years. However, some Republicans have begun to change their minds, partly spurred by the discussion over the unicameral proposal. The two-thirds vote has fostered a mentality of being a permanent minority, and in their view, allowed Democrats to escape responsibility for their actions.

"I think we lose in the public relations image every year," said Leonard. "We say we are holding out for something to fill in the blank. The public doesn't buy it. I'm almost of the opinion of saying, 'Look-it, you Democrats, there's a $12 billion problem — you want to run it? Here, you put it out by majority vote. Don't count on me to vote aye."

Then, Leonard suggests, Republicans will be in better position to run for office and become the majority party. "Do you like this? If not, vote for me."

And that suits Roberti fine. "Right now everybody can legitimately confuse the issue as where responsibility lies," said the Senate's top leader. 🏛

EXPORTING DISCONTENT

Term limits: California's gift (?) to the nation

By Charles Price and Helen Neves

Reprinted from *California Journal*, December 1991

"Restriction upon the succession of incumbents serves a rational public policy. This may deny qualified men an opportunity to serve, [but] as a general rule the overall health of the body politic is enhanced by limitations on continuous tenure. ... [The state has a legimate interest in] protecting against an entrenched, dynastic legislative bureaucracy."

— Chief Justice Malcolm Lucas, writing for the majority in *Legislature of the State of California v. March Fong Eu*, October 11, 1991.

I f those words were noise, they would be the brief hiss of a candle flame being snuffed out against a damp thumb. If they were an episode of "The Twilight Zone," they would be an unthinkable nightmare become reality. For with those words, a six-to-one majority of the California Supreme Court upheld Proposition 140. With those words, the best hope of lawmakers for political life everlasting flickered out; there would be no judicial reprieve from career-ending term limits imposed by voters in November 1990.

The Court's sweeping decision validated nearly every provision of Proposition 140, the brainchild of former Republican Los Angeles County Supervisor Pete Schabarum:

• It upheld term limits, with members of the Assembly limited to three terms or six years; senators, constitutional officers and Board of Equalization members limited to two terms or eight years.

• It agreed that Proposition 140 imposes a lifetime ban; once an elected official has "maxxed out" in a particular office, he or she may never again run for that same position.

• It upheld a provision that slashed the Legislature's budget by 40 percent.

Charles Price is a political science professor at California State University, Chico, and a frequent contributor to California Journal. Helen Neves is a doctoral student in public administration at the University of Southern California. This article is a shortened version of a paper presented by Professor Price at the National Term Limits Conference, September 1991, hosted by the Rockefeller Institute, State University of New York at Albany.

In fact, the Court only overturned that part of Proposition 140 that eliminated the state legislators' pension system.

Legislature v. Eu was the nation's first judicial test case of state legislative term limits, and the California Court's decision adds impetus to similar efforts in other states. Although the decision will be appealed to the U.S. Supreme Court, the odds that a conservative U.S. Supreme Court will overturn a decision of the conservative California Supreme Court seems unlikely.

Term limits are not new to American politics. Some states limit the number of terms their governors may serve, and the 22nd Amendment to the U.S. Constitution has limited every president since Dwight Eisenhower to two terms. But until 1990 term limits had never been imposed on state legislatures. Last year, however, first in Oklahoma and later in California and Colorado, term-limit advocates were able to qualify ballot initiatives later approved by state voters. The California ballot boasted two different term-limit initiatives in November 1990.

With the success in California, term limits became more than a local cause; it became a movement that threatened to stride colossus-like across the country. Just last month, however, the movement suffered its first setback as Washington state voters defeated what would have been the toughest term-limit measure yet. Speaker of the House Tom Foley helped spearhead the drive to defeat Washington's initiative, arguing that term limits on members of Congress would permanently eliminate the state's ability to amass seniority — and, therefore, power — and put Washington at the mercy of other states. Opponents also played upon Washingtonians' dislike for things California, pointing out that term-limits was just one more Golden State import they could do

Legislative wanna-be

Sitting legislators weren't the only ones whose futures were changed by the recent California Supreme Court ruling on Proposition 140, the term-limits initiative. The political aspirations of many legislative wanna-bes also may have ended when a six-to-one majority of the Court upheld the constitutionality of Proposition 140 last October.

In recent years, many of those wanna-bes have come from the ranks of legislative staff and others with years of behind-the-scenes training in Sacramento. Many of them intended to parlay their insider knowledge of state government into long-term careers as Assembly or Senate members.

But with Proposition 140 now firmly in place, with its limits on both legislative terms and budgets, that career path is rapidly losing its luster.

"Now," said David Takashima, chief of staff for Democratic Assemblyman Steve Peace of Rancho San Diego, "it doesn't make any sense to run for elected office."

That sentiment runs to the heart of Proposition 140, which was designed to evict incumbents and prevent would-be candidates from regarding a seat in the Legislature as the political equivalent of university tenure. Barring a successful appeal to the U.S. Supreme Court blocking term limits, 80 members of the Assembly and 40 members of the Senate will find themselves displaced in less than a decade.

While the Court has ruled that current lawmakers may keep their pensions, those elected in the future won't get that pork. That, says Takashima, is a financial burden too heavy for him to bear. "I have two young children to support, and eventually I want to send them to college," says the 41-year-

Chris Elliott is a writer with the California News Service, a project of the U.C. Berkeley graduate school of Journalism.

old, 15-year veteran of the Legislature's staff. "Without a pension, I wouldn't be able to do that."

Lobbyist Bruce Pomer, a former candidate for the Sacramento City Council, says he also has changed his mind about vying for a seat in the Legislature. Pomer, 42, who represents the Health Officers Association and is a community college trustee, last year considered launching a campaign for the Sixth Assembly District in Sacramento, now held by Democrat Lloyd Connelly. Pomer has since abandoned the idea.

"Proposition 140 wipes out any interest I'd have in running for office," he said. "I thought by some time in my career I could devote my life to public service. But you don't get good at something unless you're there for a while."

In ruling Proposition 140 constitutional, the California Supreme Court declared that it sought to "protect against entrenched, dynastic legislative bureaucracy." Sacramento consultants, however, say the Court may have inadvertently slashed the pool of qualified candidates, abandoning the Legislature to those wealthy enough to dabble in politics as a hobby.

Eventually, these consultants predict, California's Legislature — made up of the marginally employed and retired — will resemble the one that existed before 1967, when Proposition 1A created a paid, fulltime governing body.

---

without. Thus, the defeat in Washington may not have stopped the term-limit movement, merely slowed it down.

Oklahoma, Colorado, California and Washington are in the vanguard of the term-limits movement because they are initiative states, four of the 23 mainly Western states where adopting laws and/or constitutional amendments is not the exclusive province of the legislature and governor. But the movement has not caught fire everywhere. Not surprisingly, it has exhibited little clout in non-initiative states or at the federal level since few legislatures would impose term limits on themselves. It also has not fared well in initiative states where there is no provision for putting constitutional amendments on the ballot, or where initiatives rarely qualify for the ballot. Elsewhere, however, the movement is full steam ahead, and term-limits proposals soon may appear on ballots in Oregon, Montana, North Dakota and Arizona. Once again, for good or bad, California is on the cutting edge of the latest political "reform."

Why the sudden interest in term limits?

For one thing, voter frustration appears to be at an all-time high, thanks to what seems like an endless chronicle of less-than-upstanding behavior by elected officials over the last several years. At the federal level, voters have endured the Iran-Contra hearings, the savings-and-loan and banking scandals, bounced checks and other congressional "perks," finessed pay raises, negative political campaigns and the

sordid Clarence Thomas Senate confirmation hearings, among other things. At the state level, voters have been deluged with FBI sting investigations in a number of states that have uncovered considerable official corruption. In addition, partisan gerrymandering has produced professional state legislatures that are often wasteful and overstaffed. In California, the Legislature frequently is gridlocked by free-spending special interests unwilling to compromise. Thus, an increasing number of complicated issues are presented to voters via ballot initiatives. All this has helped to produce a growing anti-incumbent mood among the electorate.

Sensing this mood, national organizations such as Americans to Limit Congressional Terms, Citizens for Congressional Reform and Americans Back in Charge have taken an active role in promoting term limits as a viable reform. While these groups strive to present a bipartisan image, conservative Republicans are often their mainstays. Term limits, Republicans believe, is their best hope to wrest control of Congress and other state legislatures from Democrats.

Thus far, the impact of term limits in Oklahoma, California and Colorado has varied. In Oklahoma, political scientist Gary Copeland says that most Oklahoma legislators have given little thought to their term cap because they may serve up to 12 years, which means they may stay in office until 2002. Also, the Oklahoma Legislature is part-time and non-professional, so most lawmakers serve only a few terms

ay, "No, thanks!"

By Chris Elliott

"It's asking a lot of these candidates to take six years off, and then to have them rebuild their business after that," said Jon Kaufman, executive vice president of Solem and Associates, a San Francisco-based consulting firm. "I think Proposition 140 will discourage interest in public service and good government."

Maybe yes, maybe no. But the possibility that the pipeline of Sacramento-savvy candidates could run dry has some insiders worried.

"Where will tomorrow's legislators come from?" said Bob Schmidt, a public relations consultant in Sacramento. "It's a legitimate question, and it's a cause for grave concern."

One theory holds that local office will once again become the most important route to the Legislature. "You're not going to have the youngish, 30s, Sacramento-trained people running for office any more," says Tony Quinn, a political consultant for Braun Ketchum Public Relations and a former Republican legislative staffer.

In addition, Quinn and other consultants say, members of school boards, city councils or supervisorial boards — particularly women — who never aspired to more ambitious office before term limits are now likely to see a stint in Sacramento as an option.

Anecdotal evidence suggests, however, that neither local officeholders nor legislative staffers who want to take advantage of the legislative housecleaning are prepared to commit themselves just yet. Their reluctance, of course, is only compounded by uncertainty about reapportionment as the courts and the Legislature struggle over where new district boundaries will be drawn.

"Proposition 140 might give me a reason not to run now and see what comes up in the future," said Hunt Braly, 36, chief of staff for GOP state Senator Ed Davis of Chatsworth. In 1990 Braly challenged incumbent GOP Assemblywoman Cathie Wright but lost in the June primary.

Because term limits give would-be candidates a fighting chance against the better-established incumbents, Braly says Proposition 140 is healthy in principle. At the same time, he adds, "It makes it easier for someone in my position not to run now because I know the opportunity will be there again."

Kim Mueller, a member of the Sacramento City Council, says she is in no hurry to trade her council seat — which is not subject to term limits — for one in the Assembly.

"At this point, I'm going to wait," she said. "If I were to run, I'd take a good, long look at it."

Mueller, 34, a former volunteer and member of the city's toxics commission, says she does not regard politics as a way to pay her bills and, as a result, is not dissuaded by Proposition 140.

"I don't dream of being in office all of my life," she said.

Nor does Sacramento City Councilman Josh Pane. After his first term on the council ends, he said, he may seek a seat in the California Senate regardless of Proposition 140.

"If you're successful before you go in, you'll be successful when you get out," said Pane, 32. "The system needs revitalization. It needs new blood. I think Proposition 140 is worth it."

---

anyway. Colorado (and Washington, had it passed) limits not only state elected officials but congressmen as well. Moreover, in Washington term limits would have applied retroactively. Thus, House Speaker Foley could have run for only one more term (1992-94) before being forced to retire. That provision gave Foley and other opponents plenty of ammunition in their successful battle to defeat the initiative. One legal question that federal courts may someday be asked to resolve regarding term limits involves congressional seniority. Since seniority is critically important in Congress, do congressional term limits in some states violate citizens' equal protection?

In California, the impact of Proposition 140 is already being felt even though term limits themselves will not take effect on present incumbent legislators until 1996. A number of legislators have been scouting out other occupations. For example, former Assembly Speaker pro Tempore Mike Roos of Los Angeles left last spring to head up an education-reform consortium in his home city. Others are casting covetous eyes toward Congress. To that end, for the first time in several decades Democratic legislative leaders did not allow senior Democratic congressmen to draw the lines of congressional districts. Legislators reserved that right for themselves, mostly to suit their own ambitions rather than protect incumbent members of Congress.

"It would be naive to think that many are not eying new congressional seats [to escape] term limits," said veteran state Senator Bill Craven, a Southern California Republican.

In addition, the legislative budget reduction of nearly 40 percent has already meant that scores of staff have been eliminated or have retired early in order to receive a generous severance payment. According to some observers, legislative staff has been seriously compromised by the exodus. As Senate Republican leader Ken Maddy noted: "It is my opinion that the political hacks on the staff of legislative leaders should have been the first to go. They would not be missed." Unfortunately, political operatives remained on staff for the most part. Those who left tended to be nonpartisan technical staff.

Proposition 140 also affected all constitutional officers except for the new elective position of insurance commissioner and state judges. For the most part, Proposition 140's limits on these officials will have a relatively minor impact on governor, lieutenant governor, attorney general or controller because there has always been an unofficial two-term tradition for these offices. Only rarely has an incumbent in one of these postions served more than two terms. (An exception is Lieutenant Governor Leo McCarthy, re-elected to a third term in 1990). However, less-visible officials such as the secretary of state, treasurer or members of the Board of Equalization will be affected because incumbents in these offices sometimes hold office for extended periods. For instance, Secretary of State March Fong Eu has held office since 1974.

In order to better understand the future impact on the California Legislature of Proposition 140, legislators were surveyed on their attitudes toward this initiative. In all, some 34 legislators (about 30 percent) responded. Whether the 34 legislator respondents were representative of the general membership generally is problematic. It is probably true that those who despised the initiative were more likely to respond than supporters of the measure. Nevertheless, the size of the sample assures a diversity of views on the subject.

• In the November 1990 general election did you support, oppose or remain neutral on Proposition 140?

	Supported	Opposed	Neutral or ?
Democrats	0	19	0
Republicans	2	7	1
Independents*	0	5	0
Total	2	31	1

(* Senator Quentin Kopp is the only independent in the Legislature, although he may be joined by Senator Lucy Killea, who has left the Democratic Party and will be running as an independent in the 1992 election. Several other legislators returned their questionnaires anonymously and did not want to be identifed personally or by party. They have been listed as independents.)

Not surprisingly, the overwhelming majority of California legislators opposed Proposition 140 and campaigned actively against it. Several legislators did not publicly oppose it because they were afraid voters would take it out on them at the polls or because, as Senator Kopp put it, "It would have been self-serving to [publicly] oppose it."

Republican Craven opposed the measure, saying that it was vindictive. He said that Proposition 140 "places legislators in the same category as felons. In their case, they have a prohibition from running, and we are prohibited for life for running for the same office."

Democratic Senator Mike Thompson said Proposition 140 was not needed because California already had term limits — "elections." Veteran Republican Assemblyman Stan Statham argued, "[under Proposition 140] you'll have two kinds of legislators: those who are learning and those who are leaving." Taking the opposite view, Republican Assemblyman Chris Chandler contended, "The only way we have of moving away from a fulltime, life-term Legislature is by the artificial means of term limitation."

Most legislators surveyed were convinced that Proposition 140 would lead to considerable internal turmoil because members will lack experience, and the massive constant turnover will make it impossible for the Legislature to work effectively.

Said Democratic Assemblyman Sal Cannella, "If we have nearly 80 new people showing up in the Assembly on the 6th of January 1996, nobody will know what they're supposed to do. There will be no continuation of government. There will be no understanding of policy or legislative tradition. What are the rules? Who is going to be the speaker or the committee chairs?"

Many legislators emphasized that it take time to learn the legislative job. Maddy stated, "It takes four to five years in the

Senate before you become a truly effective senator."

Echoing this theme, Democratic Assemblyman Rusty Areias noted: "This is a pretty complicated place — a $55-billion dollar budget, 128 different departments and agencies. [New legislators] may be able to get a few things done in their second term, and then in their third term they'll be looking around for another job."

Added Assemblyman Statham, "Only legislators who have been here awhile can stand up to the special interests."

Democratic Assemblyman Ted Lempert noted: "One of the first things I did when I first came up here was to look for members I could trust on certain issues....I wonder if I were coming here in 1996 as a new legislator, who could I turn to in the Legislature? Would I have to turn to someone in the administration?"

However, Chandler felt that expertise was overrated. "I think if we had more legislators listening to what the people want, we'd be a lot better off. Name one thing these expert legislators have come up with over the last 10 years."

Proposition 140 wasn't the only term-limit proposal last November; there was also the less-Draconian Proposition 131, a campaign-finance/term-limits initiative authored by former Democratic Attorney General John Van de Kamp.

• Did you support, oppose or take no position on Proposition 131?

	Supported	Opposed	Neutral or ?
Democrats	4	11	4
Republicans	3	7	0
Independents	2	1	2
Total	9	19	6

While there was greater support for Proposition 131 among legislators, most were strongly opposed to it as well. Its only senatorial proponent, Senator Killea, stated, "I wasn't seeking a lifelong career." While agreeing with the concept of term limits, Killea felt those imposed by Proposition 140 were too short.

"Term limits of 10 to 15 years would allow enough time for sufficient experience and would provide for more gradual changes in the members of the legislative body," Killea said.

• If Proposition 140's term limits had been in effect when you first ran for the Legislature, would you still have run?

	Yes	No	Neutral or ?
Democrats	9	7	3
Republicans	5	4	1
Independents	4	0	1
Total	18	11	5

Most legislators conceded that even if Proposition 140 had been in effect when they first ran for the Legislature, they would have run anyway. However, a substantial number indicated they wouldn't have sought legislative office.

"It was hard for me to leave the security of the attorney general's office," said Democratic Assemblyman Xavier

Becerra, who was elected in 1990.

Said Democratic Assemblywoman Delaine Easton, "I was working for a large corporation, and it would have been difficult to sacrifice the benefits and ladder-climbing opportunites for a dead-end job."

Blue collar legislator Sal Cannella noted: "I worked in a factory for 30 years before I came here. I had to give up everything when I was elected. I don't go back and pick up the 30 years of seniority I had in that job... People who own businesses or are in the professions can put those positions on hold and go back to them after they leave the Legislature. Those who favor Proposition 140 keep talking about bringing back a citizen-legislature. That's baloney. The citizen is the blue-collar person working in a factory, driving a bus or teaching school and they can't just go back to their jobs again after serving in the Legislature."

• Do you think that term limits will mean a reduction in the quality of people running for the state Legislature?

	Yes	No	Neutral or ?
Democrats	9	6	4
Republicans	2	3	5
Independents	1	1	3
Total	12	10	12

While there was sharp disagreement whether there would be fewer quality legislators in the post-Proposition 140 Legislature, many lawmakers were convinced that, as Senator Thompson put it, "There will be more wealthy people running for office because they can afford it, or retired [people] because they have the time."

Democratic Senator Barry Keene thought there would be fewer lawyer-legislators. However, Maddy predicted that private institutions such as utilities, banks, labor unions and possibly law firms will furlough people to run, thus having "their representative" in office. On the other hand, Republican Senator Marian Bergeson, who opposed term limits, said, "It would give more women a chance to get elected."

• Under Proposition 140, will the Legislature have more difficulty being a co-equal branch with the governor?

	Yes	No	Neutral or ?
Democrats	18	0	1
Republicans	7	3	0
Independents	2	1	2
Total	27	4	3

Most legislators were convinced that the Legislature would have greater difficulty standing up to the governor under Proposition 140. A few disagreed. Kopp, for instance, argued that "both legislators and governors face term limits under Proposition 140. Power will not inevitably flow to the governor and his administration." Several legislators contended, however, that to be effective as a co-equal branch, the Legislature must speak with a collective voice. But, they warned, this will be difficult with virtually no experienced legislators.

• Under Proposition 140, will the Legislature be more dependent on lobbyists?

	Yes	No	Neutral or ?
Democrats	18	0	1
Republicans	7	2	1
Independents	5	0	0
Total	30	2	2

Clearly, legislators were convinced that lobbyists who comprise the "third house" would become more influential under Proposition 140. As one legislator put it, "There are no term limits on lobbyists." And, because the Legislature is short-handed on staff, some lobbyists are already stepping into the breech by assuring legislators who "carry" their bills that the lobbyist will do all the mundane details — contacting members of the appropiate committees, furnishing expert witnesses at hearings and resolving conflicts. Although senior lobbyists will be forced to get to know the new "revolving-door" legislators, Craven noted: "Absent competent, experienced staff, the members of the Legislature must depend more heavily upon third-house information to get a grasp on the matters at hand. We will have less opportunity ... to give total analysis and research to the issues in an objective manner."

However, Chandler disagreed, saying, "This all fits into this terrible, trite, knee-jerk, business-as-usual mentality that is unfortunate. If every legislator voted as if this were his last term, this would be a better and more responsive place."

• Was reapportionment complicated this year by Proposition 140?

	Yes	No	Neutral or ?
Democrats	17	1	1
Republicans	5	3	2
Independents	2	1	2
Total	24	5	5

Most legislators agreed that Proposition 140 complicated reapportionment this year because so many state legislators were interested in running for Congress to avoid term limits. Statham noted, "For the first time in California's history, assemblymen and senators are more interested in drawing congressional lines than state legislator lines." Clearly, too, all elected officials higher up on the political foodchain will have to be warier in coming years. The ambitious below them — who, in the past, may have been content to move up the legislative ladder — may now feed their ambitions by challenging incumbents.

Craven summed up legislators' views of Proposition 140's impact by quoting Alexander Hamilton: "Nothing appears more plausible at first sight, nor more ill-founded upon close inspection." Added Craven, "When you limit a term, you also limit the interest and the feeling of responsibility in the elected official. I believe the public is best served when they hang the proverbial Sword of Damocles immediately above the legislator's temple. Legislators, in turn, then very obviously recognize that if they do not perform appropiately, the electorate will cut the cord." 🏛

Rainey

Bowler

Brown

Bronshvag

Richter

Martinez

Escutia

Bowen

Caldera

Aguiar

Baca

Weggeland

Haynes

Cla

The Propos

By Charles M. Price

Charles Price is a professor of political science at Chico State University and a frequent contributor to California Journal.

Before it ever arrived in Sacramento, the Assembly's "Class of '92" had earned a mark of distinction: It was the largest gaggle of rookie lawmakers to descend on the Capitol *en masse* since 1966 — 26, to be exact (with a 27th about to arrive thanks to a special election in Fresno).

In a typical election, about five or six new members filter out of the Assembly's 80 districts. And with barely a squad of newcomers on the scene, assimilating these few into the Assembly's archane rituals posed only minor problems for leadership. But 1992 was not exactly typical. For a variety of reasons — including anti-incumbent fever among voters, new Supreme Court-reapportioned districts, term-limits-inspired retirements and public anger over legislative scandals and deadlock — about one-third of the Assembly ended up fresh to the ways of politics, Sacramento-style.

The last time Sacramento saw anything like the Class of '92 was 26 years ago, when the 33-strong Class of '66 first wandered through Capitol halls. That election, too, came on the heels of a political revolution of sorts — a 1964 U.S. Supreme Court decision, *Reynolds v. Sims*, requiring both upper and lower houses of American state legislatures to be apportioned on the basis of population. That class was heavy with future political stars; among them Governor Pete Wilson, Secretary of State March Fong Eu, Senate President pro Tem David Roberti, Ways and Means

Snyder

Honeycutt

Knight

Takasugi

Hoge

Karnette

McDonald

Solis

Napolitano

Morrow

Goldsmith

Connolly

Bornstein

'92

40 Babies

Reprinted from *California Journal,* April 1993

chairman John Vasconcellos, former Los Angeles supervisor and term-limit guru Pete Schabarum and newly elected Los Angeles Supervisor Yvonne Brathwaite Burke.

Perhaps some members of the Class of '92 will reach the top of the political ladder, but they will have to climb using fewer rungs. For the Class of '92 is the first group of freshmen and freshwomen to be elected under Proposition 140 — the term limits initiative passed in 1990. Under that initiative, Assembly members may serve a maximum of three terms, or six years. Thus, beginning in 1996, when term limits kick in for those elected to the Assembly two years ago, some 25 to 35 new members will be elected every two years.

The Class of '92 is not unique; it's a harbinger of the future.

In some ways, the neophyte 26 are much like their veteran colleagues: Many have business backgrounds and nearly all have either attended or graduated from college. Besides business backgrounds, there is the usual legislative occupational mix of lawyers, educators and local officials.

However, in a number of other ways the Class of '92 is different than the vets. It reflects what the Assembly will look like in the near future. First, the class is divided almost equally among men and women (14 men and 12 women) and party (14 Democrats and 12 Republicans). Second, about one-fifth of the class is Latino, and for the first time in 12 years an Asian-American (Republican Nao Takasugi) has been elected to the lower house. In addition, Juanita McDonald, an African-American woman, is a member of the class. Significantly, given that any connection to the Legislature was a liability in 1992, only two new members come from legislative staff — a marked departure from the trend of recent elections when many staffers followed their bosses into seats on the floor. In addition, a larger than usual number of the new members had previously held local elective office.

As new Democrat Valerie Brown stated: "Virtually none of the new members came out of state government. They mainly come from local government, local business or community service."

Many of the newcomers are on a sort of temporary leave from family businesses — for example, Kathleen Honeycutt, Bernie Richter and Ted Weggeland. The new crop is, on average, much older than typical first-termers. Republican Assemblyman Weggeland at 29 is the youngest member, but many others are in their 40s, 50s or early 60s. The class includes a number of retirees; among them are ex-law enforcement officers Larry Bowler and Richard Rainey, ex-Air Force officer Pete Knight, former school teacher Betty Karnette, and former Ford claims agent Grace Napolitano. Finally, these appear at first blush to be commuter-legislators. None expressed immediate plans to move families to Sacramento as some career legislators have in the past.

However, the most unique aspect of the Class of '92 is that its members ran for office knowing they would have only a few terms to serve in the Assembly. Unlike Speaker Willie Brown (28 years and counting) or John Vasconcellos (26 years) these newcomers cannot become Assembly careerists. Do these new members consider politics only a temporary interlude? Are they less partisan than senior members? Will they be able to provide leadership to the Assembly in 1996? To help answer these questions, *California Journal*, well, asked the new members.

First of all, none of the newcomers said they were discouraged from running because of the six-year term limit, although a few admitted it was a factor they considered. Indeed, some said they welcomed the short stint. Because of their brief tenure, how-

ever, most newcomers expressed a strong sense of urgency.

"Voters want an end to confrontational grandstanding. They want their legislators to be problem-solvers," said Democrat Betty Karnette, who defeated veteran Republican Assemblyman Gerald Felando in November.

Republican rookie Fred Aguiar added, "This class came with the mandate that we need to get things done."

Indeed, Republican Honeycutt said she and other newcomers were appalled by the tardiness of some of the senior members for floor sessions and committee hearings. "One of the things we [frosh] are doing is coming on time for our meetings. If some of these guys [veterans] were in the business world, they would have been fired long ago for showing up late so often. There is no excuse for this," said Honeycutt.

Republican Ray Haynes argued that since time is short, members of his class are more likely to do what they think is right rather than calculate votes on the basis of getting re-elected. "Whether you serve four years or six years in the Assembly, who cares? Getting re-elected to the same office becomes less important. Term limits changes your focus to concerns about public policy."

When it comes to declaring politics a career, most of the new members consider their stint in the Capitol as temporary. None of the 26 saw politics as a new life, although a pair of Republicans and nine of the Democrats reserved the right to change their minds. Most said they expected to return to their districts after a few terms.

"I don't see myself as a politician because, quite honestly, politics is trying to please all sides," said Valerie Brown. "I'm not that kind of person."

Takagusi, who is in his 70s, said, "At my age, I didn't come up here to be a career politician."

"The people elected under Proposition 140 don't have a pension system or retirement plan," said Democrat Tom Connolly. "So, we must go back to the communities that we come from and live within the rules that we established here."

Connolly felt strongly that new members would have to guard against being swept up by the glamour of the job. "An amazing seduction occurs here," he said. "When was the last time you rode an elevator where the operator knows your name? 'Morning, Assem-

blyman Connolly!' They treat you so well here — better than in my whole life. It would be very easy to start liking this lifestyle too much."

Despite their running under a term-limit system, not all the new members are enamoured of the idea. Republicans seem to like it more, with eight of the 12 supporting the concept, two opposed and two on the cusp. Only four new Democrats support it, however, with seven opposed to term limits and three on the cusp. Nearly all thought that term limits would make members more responsive to their constituents, however.

Said Honeycutt: "I return home each weekend; I shop, go to church, and do business with people who are hurting economically. It was just yesterday that we freshmen were private citizens back in the district." The first termers, she felt, had a more acute sense of the economic problems facing average Californians.

Echoing this sentiment, Democrat Louis Caldera noted: "Much as I appreciate the talent of a lot of senior members, I realize that I've been in the `real world' more recently than they have. And, that's good. But, there are areas of legislative policy that are tremendously complex that can be learned only by experience. There is a real danger that [short-term] legislators will enact the ideas that are in vogue, but not good long-term solutions."

Republican Jan Goldsmith observed, "Right now, we have a good mix between veterans and freshmen, but this won't be the case in the future." Goldsmith worried that the power of the bureaucracy could be enhanced once term limits remove all of the veteran lawmakers.

Nearly all the members (18 of 26) agreed that term limits would have another rippling effect on the state's political system: Members of their class are more likely to challenge incumbent state senators, members of Congress and constitutional officers than were their pre-term-limits predecessors. Only one Democrat thought otherwise, while three Republicans and four Democrats weren't sure.

Thus, these freshmen think the old rule of thumb about not running against incumbents is dead. Of course, plenty of districts will come open, since all state and federal office holders from California now confront limits.

Among the newcomers, Democrats were more opinionated than the Republicans about whether or not members of the Class of '92 would jockey for power early in their careers. Seven Democrats thought it would happen, five disagreed and two wouldn't say. Among Republicans, however, only three thought it would happen, two disagreed — and seven didn't know.

Some of the freshmen thought they had discerned some jockeying within the ranks already. All were keenly aware of one inevitable fact: In all likelihood one of their classmates would be elected speaker in 1996. As Valerie Brown noted: "I'm impressed with the leadership's understanding that we [frosh] are operating within a very different time framework. We need to be prepared to take over leadership by 1996."

Not surprisingly, class distinctions began to emerge between Republicans and Democrats from day one. Democrats received better committee assignments and were assigned more imposing offices than were new Republicans. And for the most part, first-term Republicans were reconciled to these political rules of the game.

One of the most dramatic incidents for the new members came during their orientation when they were informed that because of Proposition 140 budget constraints, each would receive $25,000 less for office expenses than would veterans. The announcement caused considerable consternation and confusion within newcomer ranks, and Republican and Democratic frosh saw things differently.

"One of the things that's going to have to stop is not treating members equally," fumed Republican Bowler. "We all said, 'This isn't right. We all represent the same number of people. To cut our budgets makes us second-class assemblymen and our constituents second-class voters.'"

To quell an incipient rebellion, Assembly Rules Committee Chairman John Burton was called in to talk to the necomers. According to Bowler, "Burton went into a control mode around the perimeter of the room, bad-eyeing all the Democrats and threatening them."

Subsequently, the new Democrats were called to the speaker's office, and all 14 were later chosen as vice chairs of committees (one new Republican, Richard Rainey, also was selected

as a vice chair).

GOP frosh were not amused. As Republican Ray Haynes noted: "The leadership doesn't give a rat's tail about the freshmen. They have lined their pockets at our expense. They have hurt our constituents because they want to maintain their staffs. That's outrageous. The freshmen in the majority party did nothing about it. They were afraid of their own leadership. Of course, they got paid off for doing it. They got the vice chairmanships and extra staff through backfilling, and they stepped on Republican freshmen. We got kicked in the teeth by the majority leadership. Then they say, 'Gee whiz, why don't you like us?'"

In the end, say Republicans, rookie Democrats bailed on them by not attending the newcomer protest meeting.

"We had a real chance there to impact the Assembly and we blew it," said Bowler. "In my heart, I hope that sometime in the future we will be able to work closely with the freshmen Democrats."

From the GOP point of view, although all newcomer budgets were cut, the reductions affected mainly new Republicans because Democratic staffs could be supplemented via their vice chairmanships.

Not surprisingly, Democrats see the incident differently. Valerie Brown said that Speaker Brown's intent in naming the new Democrats as vice chairs was to accelerate the newcomers' learning and get them up to speed as rapidly as possible.

"It was a recognition upon leadership's part that in a few short years [the new members] have to be ready to run the Assembly." In a similar vein, Democrat Vivien Bronshvag noted, "There's been an effort to train and prepare us unlike any previous new class."

"The leadership has been holding our feet to the fire from the beginning," said Democrat Margaret Snyder. "When was the last time you heard of a freshman being selected a vice chair? This was well thought out by leadership."

And, according to Martha Escutia, who heads the Democrats' freshman caucus, Speaker Brown insisted that new Republicans be included in all orientations.

"One of the things I planned for new members was a mock [floor] session — it was great. The speaker encouraged me to include Republicans

from the beginning. If he had wanted to be partisan about it, he could have excluded them. After all, knowing the rules of the game helps you to win."

New Democrats were also more sympathetic with the leadership's explanation for the need to cut new members' office budgets. "I could understand the rationale for having first-termers receive less in office budget funds," said Democrat Julie Bornstein. "It was easier to cut us because we hadn't hired our staff." Refuting GOP claims that the vice chairmanships helped provide extra staff, Bornstein said, "None of us have received any extra staff because of our vice chairmanships."

Finally, Democrat Joe Baca argued that it was the Republicans who fired the first partisan shot in the 1993 session. "I thought the speakership election would be the time for everyone to get together and show bipartisan spirit," he said. "The Republicans initially didn't even have a candidate in mind. Their vote for [Minority Leader Jim] Brulte was just a protest vote. That's not cooperation."

"I don't have any doubt that we will be more than willing to make independent choices and not follow our parties' lock-step," said Valerie Brown, a notion echoed by Republican Rainey.

"I've found that when we get together with the Democratic freshmen we have a lot in common," he said. "We're in agreement on about 85 percent of the issues. I think we are going to make an impact."

Perhaps it is expecting too much to believe that 26 rookies will become something like a new "Gang of 26" and seriously challenge their respective leaderships in the first weeks of the session. After all, they have just barely completed their orientation. They are, first and foremost, Republicans and Democrats, not first-termers.

To their credit, the Assembly frosh have successfully pressured their more senior colleagues into greater punctuality, and this is a good symbolic first step. However, major changes in the way the Assembly operates probably won't come for a year or two, or until the seniors depart.

As Democratic rookie Caldera observed: "Any institution resists change. It's natural. When the seniors are gone, it will be easier to take on some of the sacred cows."

LOBBYING & INTEREST GROUPS

The Political Reform Act of 1974 helped reshape relations between lobbyists and legislators. Prior to enactment of this proposition, legislative advocates spent a great deal of time and money entertaining lawmakers and thus winning their favor (and their votes). But the 1974 act prohibited a legislator from taking more than $10 a month from a lobbyist, barred lobbyists from "arranging" for campaign contributions from their clients (this provision has since been invalidated by the courts), established extensive and detailed expense and income reporting requirements, and established the Fair Political Practices Commission to implement the law. The measure has been reasonably successful in cutting the entertainment tie between legislators and advocates and began modifying the way of life in the Capitol. Actually, the system had started to change in 1966 when the Legislature became a full-time body. Many lawmakers and lobbyists brought their families to Sacramento, reducing time available for socializing.

The system today is a far cry from the 1930's and 40's when the late Artie Samish boasted: "To hell with the Governor of California! I'm the Governor of the Legislature." And the state's archetypical lobbyist then was probably right. In his long reign, hardly a bill passed the Legislature without Samish's approval. He raised about $1 million over a six-year period from a nickel-a-barrel levy on beer provided by his biggest client and spent it getting legislators "elected and un-elected," as he liked to put it. Until 1953 when he was convicted for income-tax evasion, Samish was dominated Sacramento; other lobbyists were virtually powerless by comparison. Samish's downfall began when he was interviewed for Collier's magazine and posed with a ventriloquist's dummy he called "Mr. Legislature." The resulting embarrassment prodded the Legislature to pass a mild "reform act" technically banning lobbying and regulating "legislative advocates" in Sacramento. But if the activities of lobbyists are not as blatant as in Samish's day, their power continues unabated. Indeed, the increasing costs of running for election — campaigning for a hotly contested Assembly seat can cost more than $1 million — has made lobbyists and the firms that employ them more important than ever. Moreover, the Legislature in recent years has been plagued with a new round of scandals set off by a "sting" operation run by the FBI and the U.S. attorney's office. State Senator, Democrat Joseph Montoya of Whittier, resigned his office after being convicted of taking $3,000 to help secure passage of the FBI's phony legislative proposal, a bill that would have subsidized a shrimp-packing plant on the Sacramento River. State Board of Equalization member Paul Carpenter, a Los Angeles Democrat and former Senator, and two legislative staff members were also been convicted in the "sting." And a third Senator, Alan Robbins, resigned and plead guilty to corruption and is serving time in prison. In the Spring of 1993 Senator Frank Hill and Assemblyman Pat Nolan, both Republicans, lobbyist Clay Jackson and another staff member were indicted as well.

Types of lobbyists

While a few big-name lobbyists who represent stables of clients receive most of the publicity, the corps of advocates includes almost every interest group in the state. In 1993 nearly 900 advocates are registered. They fall into several categories:

- *Contract lobbyists.* These advocates will work for almost any client willing to pay their fee. The most successful of them charge high prices, make substantial campaign contributions and get results.
- *Corporation and trade association lobbyists.* These advocates work for one company and represent only the interests of their firms, although they often work in tandem with other lobbyists trying to reach the same goal.
- *Public agency lobbyists.* Aside from the associations representing public agencies, numerous cities, counties and special districts maintain their own representatives in Sacramento. And most state agencies have "legislative liaisons," though they are not required to register.
- *"Brown-bag" lobbyists.* These advocates represent interests seeking reforms in a variety of so-called public-interest fields. They include numerous organizations with budgets sufficient only for bag lunches.

Lobbying process

Lobbyists operate in several ways. They provide information and arguments on pending legislation in an attempt to win legislators to their point of view. This information function is a legitimate part of the Legislature's work as it helps define issues. Lobbyists also establish friendships with legislators. In addition some lobbyists contribute substantial amounts to campaigns and entertain lavishly on behalf of their clients. Many lobbyists orchestrate appeals from their membership at the local level such as letter-writing campaigns and political participation. Lobbyists also lobby the governor, the bureaucracy, regulatory commissions, the courts and the public.

Lobbyists can succeed because there are a great many bills considered each year about which lawmakers have relatively little knowledge or interest, and a word from a lobbyist may tip the balance. A smart lobbyist knows he or she is wasting time trying to persuade a legislator who has a firm philosophical commitment to one side or another on an issue, and so focuses on the uncommitted lawmaker.

All legislators are susceptible to persuasion by representatives of interest groups. But some are more attuned, for example, to corporate spokesmen, while others are more apt to go along with a representative of an environmental organization. Unlike the Samish days, when the public did not get a clear picture of the happenings in Sacramento, the pleading of teams of the Capitol's most powerful and persuasive advocates now occasionally fall on deaf ears when legislators got a clear message from their constituents. While lobbyists tend to come from within government ranks — i.e., legislators and ex-staff — members retiring from the Legislature because of Proposition 112 of June 1990 must wait one year before going into lobbying. Proposition 112 also prohibits honoraria, limits acceptance of gifts, and restricts compensation for appearing before a state agency. 🏛

Lobbying has been an accepted part of the legislative process for years, its practicioners known as the "third house" of the Legislature. But in recent years, due mainly to the ever-increasing cost of political campaigns, the role of the lobbyist has changed. They have always influenced the legislative process, but with the escalating costs of campaigns, they've become the major conduit for money that politicians need to be reelected. This issue of *California Journal* examines aspects of the lobbying industry, including its most

successful firms, a handful of prominent lobbyists and the expansion of lobbying's underground and the way government lobbies itself.

If lobbying is the art of persuasion, it just may be the healthiest art form in Sacramento. The number of groups and firms employing paid persuaders has nearly tripled in the past 10 years so that nearly 1700 organizations now have some form of representation in Sacramento. The amount spent on lobbying has increased even faster, probably exceeding $70 million for 1985. In 1975 only $20 million per year was spent on lobbyists.

In part this reflects the growth of state government itself; the California state budget has almost tripled during that same period. But it also reflects an increased recognition that decisions made by the state — in the Legislature and in a myriad of state agencies — have substantial impacts on a growing number of businesses and professions. Even other government agencies now find the need for a Sacramento advocate to protect their share of the state's largess. This aspect of lobbying's growth doesn't alarm most observers. Indeed, it can be seen as a healthy participation in the governmental process.

Warping the system

However, the growth of the lobbying industry has also coincided with another phenomenon — the rapidly escalating cost of election campaigns. And the connection between the two, in the view of many, has become so pervasive that it is beginning to warp the system with an unholy alliance between private interests, who view lobbying expenses

and campaign contributions as business investments, and legislators, who see in lobbyists and special interests a ready source of the campaign cash needed for reelection.

In recent years the trend has produced the "bag bill" — a measure introduced and perhaps pursued solely to leverage campaign contributions out of special interests. Proposals that often start out with a noble purpose end up, conveniently, as a kind of Brinks truck filled with campaign cash.

The most notable current example is a proposal to change the state's "uni-

THE PERSUADERS

LOBBYING — AN ART FORM FLOURISHING IN SACRAMENTO

Reprinted from *California Journal*, February 1986

By RICHARD ZEIGER

LOBBYING TOTALS: 1975-1986

YEAR	#LOBBYISTS	#EMPLOYERS	TOTAL $ SPENT
1975-76	630	795	40,018,666
1977-78	582	760	49,656,908
1979-80	613	857	59,023,150
1981-82	638	1041	58,345,176
1983-84	753	1338	112,519,158
1985-86	838	1695	137,594,247
1987-88	825	1544	158,498,208
1989-90	817	1537	193,578,059
1991-92	886	1455	116,465,129
1993-94	1021	1568	- -

tary" method of taxing foreign corporations that operate in California. Many corporations, both foreign and domestic, found they had something to gain or lose from this proposal and thus unleashed an army of lobbyists armed with the promise of campaign riches. Indeed, the proposal has proved so lucrative for lawmakers' campaign accounts — not to mention the bank accounts of the Capitol lobbying corps — the suspicion is widespread that the matter is unsettled because no one wants to give up an easy source of money.

A part of the process

Even those who deny that contributions matter — most notably Assembly Speaker Willie Brown, who has been accused by some of allowing the bag bill to flourish — concede they are expected from those who can afford them. In a recent *California Journal* interview, Brown maintained that the vast amount of money given by special interests "cancel each other out," adding that he could not remember a single instance when contributions made the difference in the outcome of a bill. But Brown noted that his Assembly members "have to get reelected. They've got to get the dough from someplace." The logical source is those who want to play the legislative game.

The change has affected not only legislators, but the business community as well. Businesses have accepted that campaign contributions are just another part of the process. According to

one lobbyist, there used to be a time when at least some businesses resisted contributing "under the gun." That has almost disappeared. Furthermore, the amount of money involved is going up.

"Once, if you contributed $20,000, spread among a number of legislators over two years, that was a lot. Now, it's $70,000 or $80,000 per year for one person," the lobbyist added.

Walter Zelman, lobbyist for the consumer group Common Cause, believes the mining of campaign contributions from lobbyists "has tainted the process" and that the problem lies with the system and not with so-called corrupt individuals.

But campaign contributions are becoming a relatively blunt instrument; just about everyone expects them and, at least for the Legislature's biggest fund raisers, they no longer leave a lasting impression. As a result, lobbyists have begun developing more sophisticated ways of reaching legislators.

Lobbyists, of course, are more than conduits for campaign contributions (although for some, the ability to influence how, when and where a client contributes creates an enormous amount of leverage with legislators). Lobbyists also devise strategies for moving bills through the legislative process, work with clients and/or employers to influence bills through grass-roots efforts in lawmakers' districts, manage professional associations and public-relations campaigns for clients and develop a diverse set of contacts in all branches of state government.

In the past few years, businesses have also begun hiring platoons of lobbyists to push for a measure. Although one individual or firm may be in charge, it is not uncommon to subcontract out some of the lobbying work to specialists who might have good contact with one crucial legislator. This has created new opportunities for former legislators or staff members to enter the lobbying profession where they can take advantage of the personal friendships — all to the benefit of their new employers.

Also emerging in recent years is the combination firm employing both lawyers, lobbyists and even public-relations specialists. These firms offer a "complete service" to their clients. The changes needed in the law can be researched, lawmakers contacted and a publicity campaign mounted if necessary.

The combination of an increasingly professional lobbying corps, backed by the money to fuel election campaigns, is proving to be almost overwhelming. At times it threatens to unbalance the governmental system. Although legislative staff is large enough to provide an objective look at pending legislation, there is little in the way of political balance.

Zelman notes that his type of public interest lobbyist can have some impact, even without campaign contributions. "But we can't compete in sheer numbers. In some fields there are 30 or 40 private-interest lobbyists for every public-interest lobbyist," he said.

This imbalance, in recent years, has resulted in the Legislature regularly appearing to be at the beck-and-call of special interests. Indeed, the only time you see a good old-fashioned fight these days is when two large special interests square off.

Zelman and other reformers — most of whom favor some form of public campaign financing — see the solution in reforming the campaign financing system so that lawmakers will not have to turn to special interest lobbies for money. "The solution is to make it easier to raise money, not more difficult. Then they can worry about the things they are supposed to worry about," Zelman offered. 🏛

illustration by Buz Walker Teach

POWER TO THE TEACHERS

The influential California Teachers Association disproves the old adage: In Capitol politics, those who can, teach.

By Steve Scott

"**T**hose that do teach young babes Do it with gentle means and easy tasks..."
—*William Shakespeare*

The hard-working, selfless teacher, toiling against adversity to bring the light of learning into young minds. It's an ideal firmly embedded in our history and culture — "the Lord's work" in an enlightened society. Thinking about teachers conjures images of Socrates, unlocking the mysteries of thought and logic merely by posing questions to his hero-worshiping students. Or Annie Sullivan, unlocking the very consciouness of Helen Keller with gentle patience and tough love. RobinWilliams in "Dead Poet's Society"; Sidney Poitier in "To Sir With Love"; Robert Donat (or Peter O'Toole) in

Steve Scott is a radio commentator and editor of State Capitols Report.

"Goodbye, Mr. Chips."

With icons like these, one would think teachers have more than a leg up in the public-relations department. So what were the descendants of all those shining lights doing at a San Diego resort last summer, sitting in workshops on grass-roots organizing and voter contact at something called the "Political Action Institute?" They were learning about what, for many teachers, has become as essential as an education degree — political activism.

Sponsoring the institute was an organization that has become, arguably, the most politically influential labor union in the state — the 240,000-member California Teachers Association. Over the past eight years, CTA has doled out more than $3 million in legislative campaign contributions and spent more than $10 million to support or oppose various initiatives. Moreover, CTA has built an unparalleled organizational machine, capable of mobilizing its members on short notice for everything from strike support to political rallies.

Supporters of the CTA say the union is using its clout to wage a valiant struggle to preserve adequate funding for schools. Democratic Assemblywoman Delaine Eastin of Union City, who chairs the Assembly Education Committee, says that "when they're lobbying for or against education issues, it's not just 'what's good for our union?' It's 'what's good for the kids?'"

Critics, however, say the CTA is no different in its exercise of political power than any other special interest group. "There can be some argument made," says Ruth Holton, executive director of California Common Cause, "that because of [CTA's] clout in the Legislature, it is harder for other groups that are just as deserving to get their message heard."

Complaints about the political sway held by the teachers' unions are nothing new; they've been uttered ever since the California Teachers Association formed in 1865. For most of its 128-year history, CTA had a fairly loose admission policy, and a number of administrators were counted among its membership. In the early 1970s the administrators were kicked out, and the organization became involved in the fight over collective bargaining.

At the time, most of CTA's energies were spent competing for members with its arch-rival — the 75,000-member California Federation of Teachers.

But in 1978 the battle for bargaining rights quickly took a back seat to a more immediate, common threat — passage of the property tax-slashing Proposition 13. Although it had formed a political action committee, CTA's scattered and disorganized operation was no match for the initiative's juggernaut, according to Ed Foglia, who in 1978 was beginning the first of two terms as CTA president.

"We came to understand," says Foglia, "that politics is not just a publicity campaign. Politics is door-to-door — the kinds of things that you have to do in order to win elections."

Foglia says he helped develop a "Blueprint for Political Action," — a centralized system of data retrieval, voter registration, absentee canvassing and extensive member education. The political organization tightened and a statewide lobbying and campaign infrastructure began to take shape. That process was hastened in 1983 with the arrival of Alice Huffman as director of government relations. Huffman, an ally of Assembly Speaker Willie Brown, says she "politicized" the organization, helping it to better use its power to influence policy. "I had to teach them that they could do the right thing *and* be successful," says Huffman.

With it's campaign apparatus firmly in place, and a $5 per year assessment on each member's dues for political action, CTA began creeping up the list of heavyweight donors to legislative races, from fifth place in 1985-86 to fourth in 1987-88. In 1989-90 the California Teachers Association's PAC was the Number One legislative campaign donor, giving more than $1 million. In 1991-92 it was in a virtual tie for second with the California Correctional Peace Officers Association, giving just under $900,000.

While contributions at this level automatically make CTA a player, most inside and outside the union mark the turning point in its power and influence to 1988 and the campaign for Proposition 98. The initiative, which guaranteed that schools receive at least 40 percent of the state's general fund budget, was a pent-up response to the erosion in school funding that started with Proposition 13 and continued through George Deukmejian's tenure as governor (1983-90). CTA spent millions to qualify and campaign for Proposition 98, and benefited from the support of state schools chief Bill Honig,

then one of the state's more popular political figures.

When Proposition 98 eked out its narrow victory, schools — and the CTA — found themselves in a unique position. After a decade fighting for funds with the rest of the budget "have-nots," schools were now seen as the biggest "haves" of them all. Almost immediately, they were in court, battling a coalition of children's advocates over whether on-campus health, nutrition, welfare and immunization services would be counted under the 40 percent guarantee.

"Before 98 passed, they went out and asked child-development groups to join them," says Steve Barrow with the Children's Advocacy Institute. "After 98 passed, they sued to remove the child-development programs from underneath Prop 98 protections, putting about $300 million of programs for the most high-risk kids at risk." Ultimately, the state Supreme Court ruled against CTA, and added the programs to the guarantee.

If CTA's relationship with other public advocacy groups is occasionally cool, its relationship with the state's Republican governor is openly hostile. Responding to the pressures of back-to-back budget chasms, Governor Pete Wilson proposed suspending Proposition 98. He also proposed that the age for kindergarten entry be delayed six months. CTA responded with an unprecedented, million-dollar, off-year ad campaign. "We felt it was better to let the public speak, rather than us," said Huffman. "If you have the public joining in, to us it offered more leverage."

The spot, which featured a tearful child being turned away from kindergarten, was heavy-handed but effective, and Wilson backed off the proposal, even though he insisted it was similar to a union-backed plan of a few years ago. The practical effect of the flap was that CTA became "Public Enemy Number One" within the Wilson administration.

"They told a big lie to tell a second big lie, to try to convince people that we had cut school funding," said Maureen DiMarco, Wilson's secretary of Child Development and Education.

CTA officials maintain their actions before and since the passage of Proposition 98 are motivated by a simple and basic instinct — survival. "It's politically popular in this state, right now, to put us in competition with welfare,"

CALIFORNIA GOVERNMENT & POLITICS ANNUAL

CTA'S SACRAMENTO GATEKEEPER

Well connected and tenacious, Alice Huffman helps keep teachers in lawmaker's faces

One could almost hear the smile on Del Weber's face through the telephone line as a reporter wrapped up a lengthy interview. "When," wondered the California Teachers Association's Republican president, "are you going to ask me about Alice Huffman?"

It is impossible to talk about the rise in prominence of the CTA without also, in the same breath, mentioning Huffman — the union's 56-year-old political director. Based in Sacramento, Huffman directs all aspects of CTA's political strategy, from educating and organizing local members to coordinating statewide initiative efforts.

"She is *the* major force behind CTA's political clout," says Common Cause's Ruth Holton. "She is a very important behind-the-scenes political figure here in California."

Huffman says she didn't seek a career in politics, but rather "politics came to me." A high school dropout, she went to work in 1966 on the campaign of Michigan Congressman Carl Stokes. Urged to move to California "to get a free education," Huffman says she was accepted at UC Berkeley and graduated in two years. She eventually ended up working for Jerry Brown as a deputy in the Parks and Recreation Department.

In 1980 Huffman was invited to join a group being formed by the new Assembly speaker, Willie Brown. The organization was the Black American Political Association of California. "BAPAC caught my fancy more than most of the Blacks working in [Jerry] Brown's administration at the time," says Huffman. "It just seemed to have such promise."

Huffman's ties with Speaker Brown through BAPAC gave her the connections she needed to land a job as a lobbyist with the CTA in 1983. Within a year, she was running the government relations division, and not long after that, CTA's political action committee began showing up among the top campaign donors in the state.

Eventually, Huffman stopped lobbying and began focusing entirely on the political organization. She helped mobilize the coalition that passed Proposition 98 and directed the very successful off-year media campaign last year against Governor Pete Wilson's budget proposals. She also built a "continuing education" program in politics for rank-and-file teachers.

"The biggest thing they do is the Political Action Institute," says Lynne Faulks, president of the Mount Diablo Education Association. "It empowers teachers to go back home, be politically active and make a difference."

As a tough, no-nonsense operative, Huffman has few peers in Sacramento. "If you're thin-skinned, you don't belong in this business," she says. "There's no way you can work in politics and not acquire enemies." However, her skill and tenacity have also won her fierce loyalty among her CTA colleagues. "She was my only ally at one time on Proposition 98," recalls former CTA President Ed Foglia. "I have a lot of respect for her."

"She's a jewel," gushes Weber.

Perhaps Huffman's closest political association — and her most controversial — is with Willie Brown. Critics of the union charge that Huffman is a conduit through which the speaker distributes campaign money to Democrats.

"[CTA] is a partisan arm of Willie Brown, and that's because of the connection between Willie and Alice," says Maureen DiMarco, Wilson's secretary of Child Development and Education and herself a Democrat.

Lately, these criticisms have been fueled by Huffman's personal crusade to push Brown as a candidate for governor. The effort, which involves gathering petition signatures on Brown's behalf, became immediate fodder for political reporters, and the reaction caught both Huffman and her superiors by surprise.

"All of us were caught up short by the realization that, in today's CTA, you don't have a private life," says Weber, who maintains the Brown campaign has no connection — official or unofficial — with the union.

Huffman insists her campaign for Brown has both a substantive and symbolic value. "No African-American name ever floats for constitutional office," she says. "Willie Brown is the most qualified of all the names floating around. Why not give him a chance?"

As for the broader criticisms of her alliance with Brown, Huffman dismisses them as sour grapes. "They [Republican business interests] used to have a monopoly, but now we're at the table, too. And we have something else they don't — a teacher in every legislative district."

— Steve Scott

says CTA President Del Weber. "We're not in competition with welfare. All we're saying is, 'Let's at least hold even with where we are now.'"

The union also points out that it is far from alone in the fight to preserve school funding. Other education organizations, including those representing school boards, administrators and classified employees, have joined CTA and CFT in what's been dubbed "The Unusual Coalition."

"The relationship is very professional," says Davis Campbell, executive director of the California School Boards Association. "There's a real committment to try and stay together as much as possible around that single issue [school funding]."

While the perception of unity among education groups is important, it is CTA's political operation that really gets the job done for teachers. In addition to its deep contribution pockets, the union has one of the most sophisticated grass-roots operations going. Union locals can be mobilized on short notice to man phone banks, walk precincts or host news conferences.

"What makes CTA strong is 'people power,'" says Huffman. "Legislators know that, when they go home, it's teachers they'll be talking to."

According to political consultant Steve Hopcraft, "CTA has the top political operation in the state."

Most of the politicians who benefit from this strong operation are Demo-

crats. "The joke in our caucus is that they're a leisure time subsidiary of the Democratic Party," says Glendale Republican Assemblyman Pat Nolan. "If you deviate from their orthodoxy, they have a tremendous amount of money to pour into your district and tell the voters

that you hate children."

The numbers tell the story. Only three Republican Senate candidates running in 1992 got money from CTA. In the 80 Assembly races, only eight GOP candidates received money from CTA. And only one Republican — Assemblywoman Doris Allen — got the union's self-imposed maximum of $15,000. All told, more than 90 percent of all the money CTA gave last year went to Democrats.

CTA officials counter the charge of partisanship by pointing to their president, Del Weber, who is a Republican from Orange County. Weber says Republican candidates for office get a fair hearing, but he admits to a substantial philosophical divergence between the union and the GOP.

"When you look at the platforms of the two parties," says Weber, "the Democrats tend to vote for things which are better for public education, and they tend to get our endorsements. The Republicans tend not to [vote for public education], and so they tend not to get our endorsements." Huffman adds another point of departure: The GOP's distain for unions. "Ninety percent of the Republicans we interview have a problem with collective bargaining," she says.

The above responses from Weber and Huffman point to the central paradox of the CTA, one that shades its relations not just with the Legislature but with the rest of the education community. On one hand, it is an advocacy organization, seen by many in the public to be fighting the good fight for kids in the classroom. On the other, it is a union, with a clearly defined mandate to represent the interests of teachers. Clearly, CTA benefits from its image as a selfless advocate for education, but where does one role end and the other begin?

For CTA and its supporters, there is no conflict — what's good for teachers is good for schools. "They are a special-

interest group, but every group sees its interests as `special,'" says Eastin. "Some of us see that when your special interest is children and education, you're more on the side of the angels."

Mary Bergan, president of the rival California Federation of Teachers,

vehemently rejects the suggestion that a union identity precludes doing well by students. "I think there are people who would like to think so," says Bergan, "but I don't think that's the case."

To its political adversaries, however, CTA is no less narrow in its focus than doctors, lawyers, insurance companies and all the other "black hat" lobbying interests in Sacramento. "Teachers' salaries are important, but not when you don't have immunization; when you don't have health care; when you don't have basic nutrition," says Barrow of the Children's Advocacy Institute. "They're so protective of their tribe that they've lost sight of the impact [their actions] have on kids."

DiMarco, herself a Democrat, puts it more bluntly: "They're a labor organization, and should not be mistaken for an educational organization."

The one area where supporters and opponents agree is that, ultimately, CTA's success as an institution will be measured not by how many legislators it gets elected, but by the contribution it makes to improving the environment in schools.

"CTA is going to have to have an impact on the workplace," observes Foglia. "Teachers will say [to the union], 'If you're so successful in other areas, how about on a day-to-day basis?' CTA is going to have to continue to evolve in that direction, or else they could very well go down the way other unions have." 🏛

PARTIES, POLITICS & ELECTIONS

Political Parties

By both design and tradition, political parties in California are exceptionally weak — especially when compared to the machine politics prevalent in some eastern states. The weakening of the party structure was engineered by Hiram Johnson and the Progressives starting in 1911 as a reaction to the machine politics of the railroad interests and San Francisco boss Abe Ruef. Parties were explicitly forbidden from endorsing in non-partisan contests and implicitly from making pre-primary endorsements in partisan contests for much of this century. All local offices and judgeships were made nonpartisan, and a unique method of running, called cross-filing, was instituted. Numerous provisions were written into the law for the express purpose of reducing party power, and many of these restrictions remain in the law today. An independent spirit was fostered in California, and even now there are parts of the state where the electorate pays very little attention to a candidate's party. It is these areas — notably the San Joaquin Valley and the rural districts that can hold the balance of power in state elections.

Under cross-filing, which lasted from 1914 to 1959, a candidate could file for the nomination of not only his or her own party but other parties as well (and until 1952, without any indication of party affiliation). This had the effect of weakening party structure and making pressure groups and the press more important. It also led to the election of popular candidates in the primary, when they won both the Republican and Democratic nominations. Generally, cross-filing helped Republicans more than Democrats, and it is probably significant that Democrats have done much better in elections since the system was eliminated in favor of traditional primaries.

California now has six official parties — Democratic, Republican, Libertarian, Peace and Freedom, American Independent, and as of 1992, the Green Party. A party can win official status by getting the signatures of one percent of the registered voters or by obtaining a petition signed by a number of voters equal to ten percent of the votes cast for governor in the previous election. To remain official, a party must get two percent of the vote for a statewide candidate and retain one-15th of one percent of registered voters. Loss of official status means that a party can run candidates by write-in only, a difficult assignment in an era of electronic voting.

Party organization

The party structure is spelled out in detail in state law, although some minor variations are allowed for Democrats and Republicans. These are the basic official elements of party structure:

• *National committee members.* These are elected by the delegation to the national convention and serve as the state party's representatives on the national committee of each party.

• *Delegates to national convention.* Slates are developed by supporters of each primary candidate, and winning delegates — with alterations and additions — cast the state's votes at the quadrennial convention. The winner-take-all primary is used by California Republicans. State Democrats use a proportional representation system of delegates elected from congressional districts.

• *County central committees.* These committees, elected directly by the voters, are charged with directing party affairs in each county. In fact, however, these committees are weak, and the real power is held by the office-holders in each county.

• *State central committee.* This committee is comprised of about 1400 members in the GOP and 2500 to 3000 members in the Democratic Party. This committee is charged with electing party officials, managing and operating the party, and selecting presidential electors. An executive committee of the state central committee handles the day-to-day operation of the party.

• *State chairman.* In theory, the chairman speaks for the party and develops election strategy in conjunction with the executive committee. With rare exception, however, the main leaders are the major office holders of both parties.

As noted, Progressive reforms weakened party organization in the state. However, several new developments may serve to strengthen California parties:

1) Because of court rulings in the 1980s, parties may now make endorsements in partisan primaries. (They are still prohibited from endorsing in non-partisan contests.) Democrats have established detailed regulations for their party on their endorsing rules and format. Republicans have decided, because of potential divisions, not to endorse. Since 1988, (the first year that endorsing went into effect), endorsing has not been a major factor influencing the nomination or election politics of the Democratic Party, but it could evolve into a significant factor in the years ahead.

2) Parties have democratized selection to State Central Committees. There are fewer appointments by office-holders, and more elections from the counties. Democrats have created Assembly District Caucuses in the 80 districts to choose 12 delegates per district.

3) Lastly, election by Democrats of Jerry Brown (former governor and ambitious elective office seeker) symbolized the growing importance of the state chair's position. Current state chairs are Bill Press for the Democrats and Tirso del Junco for the Republicans.

DEMOCRATIC and REPUBLICAN PARTY ORGANIZATION

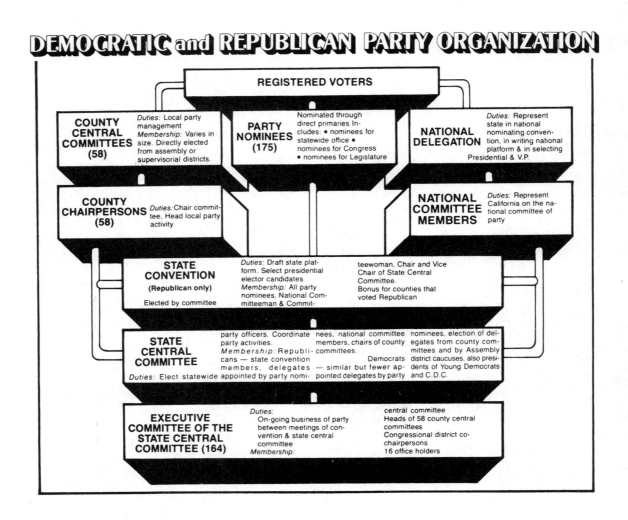

Elections

A person may register to vote in California who is 18, a citizen of the United States and a resident of the county of registration for at least 30 days prior to the election (and who is otherwise not disqualified, such as in the case of certain felons). There are several types of elections in California:

• *State primaries.* These take place the first Tuesday after the first Monday in June of even-numbered years. At these elections, nominees for national, state and some local offices are selected. Usually, there are a number of propositions also on the ballot.

• *State general elections.* These take place on the first Tuesday after the first Monday in November of even-numbered years, and voters make their selections from among the nominees chosen in the primaries. The ballot usually contains more propositions.

• *Special elections.* These rarely take place on a state-wide basis because of high cost, although there was one in November 1973 when Governor Ronald Reagan put his tax-limitation initiative to a vote (it lost). Special elections are more often held locally to fill vacancies in Congress and the state Legislature. These are different from most other elections in that the voters are given a list of candidates of all parties. If no one candidate receives a simple majority, a runoff is held four weeks later among the top vote-getters in each party. In some cases, this means that candidates far down the list make the runoff while the candidate who finished second in number of votes does not.

• *Local elections.* Often, elections for local city council and special district-director posts are not consolidated with the primary and general elections and are held at various times during the year.

Political History

During the early years of state history, there were rapid political swings based on economics. When things went well, the big-business interests were in control. During a depression period in the 1870s, the Workingmen's Party under Denis Kearney of San Francisco came to power and managed to get much of its program enacted. When prosperity returned, the party disappeared. Economic and political power went into the hands of the "Big Four" — railroad magnates Charles Crocker, Mark Hopkins, Collis P. Huntington and Leland Stanford. Southern Pacific dominated California politics from the 1880s until the advent of the Progressives more than 25 years later.

The Progressives

Republican newspaper editors started in the first decade of this century to drum up opposition to the railroads and the boss of San Francisco, Abe Ruef. Disgruntled Republicans started the Lincoln-Roosevelt league, and graft-fighter Hiram Johnson became the group's candidate for governor. He pledged to kick Southern Pacific out of the Republican Party and out of California government. He won easily and immediately started enacting reforms such as the initiative, referendum, recall, cross-filing, civil service, and a multitude of other programs. Johnson went to the United States Senate in 1916 and was succeeded by another progressive, William D. Stephens. The movement lost its force in the 1920s as postwar prosperity produced political apathy. Until the next depression, the regular Republicans maintained control of state government.

The Great Depression resulted in the 1934 gubernatorial candidacy of muckraking author Upton Sinclair (his slogan: "End Poverty in California") with his radical plan for reforming the economic system. Republican Frank Merriam defeated Sinclair by about a quarter of a million votes. With the Democrats riding high nationally under President Franklin D. Roosevelt, the Republicans finally lost the governorship in 1938 to state Senator Culbert Olson.

Four years later, a new progressive era began under Earl Warren. Aided by cross-filing, the former Alameda County district attorney and state attorney general portrayed himself as a non-partisan official — an image he embroidered later as an activist Chief Justice of the United States. Warren's personal popularity was unprecedented in California political history. He was able to push most of his programs through the Legislature (with a compulsory health-insurance plan the notable exception). Warren was the Republican vice-presidential nominee in 1948 (with Thomas Dewey) and perhaps could have remained governor indefinitely. After 10 years as the state's chief executive, he was named U.S. chief justice by President Eisenhower in 1953.

The new governor was Goodwin J. Knight, who was reelected in his own right in 1954 but was unable to establish himself as leader of the Republican Party because he had to contend with two other major figures, then-Vice-President Richard Nixon and U.S. Senator William Knowland. In 1958, Knowland decided that for political and personal reasons — he thought being governor was a better stepping stone to the presidency — he would leave his safe Senate seat to run for governor. Knight was pushed aside and virtually forced to run for Knowland's seat. Knowland embraced a right-to-work initiative, setting the stage for a massive Democratic victory led by the gubernatorial candidate, Edmund G. (Pat) Brown. Nixon, defeated in a 1960 run for president against John F. Kennedy, tried an unsuccessful comeback by running against Brown in 1962.

In his second term, Brown became embroiled in a bitter intra-party fight with the powerful speaker of the Assembly, Jesse M. Unruh, and elected to seek a third term rather than give his arch-rival a clear shot at his job. In the primary election, Brown's forces concentrated on shooting down the moderate Republican candidate, former San Francisco Mayor George Christopher, preferring to run against the conservative Ronald Reagan, a former actor. Somebody goofed: Reagan crushed Brown in the general by a million votes.

Democratic nominee Unruh tried to unseat Reagan four years later. Although plagued by limited financial resources, Unruh cut Reagan's victory margin in half. Reagan kept his 1966 pledge not to seek a third term in 1974, leaving the gates wide open. Twenty-nine candidates ran in the primary, with Brown's son, Jerry, and Houston I. Flournoy emerging from the pack to represent the Democratic and Republican parties in November. Brown won by only 179,000 votes, almost blowing his big early lead. Four years later, he rebounded with a 1.3-million-vote victory over the GOP attorney general, Evelle J. Younger.

In 1982 Jerry Brown continued the two-term limit tradition and ran for U.S. Senator (he lost to San Diego Mayor Pete Wilson, a Republican). Attorney General George Deukmejian won a tough primary against Lieutenant Governor Mike Curb for the Republican party nomination and squeaked past the Democratic candidate, Los Angeles Mayor Tom Bradley, in November.

In a repeat in 1986, Deukmejian trounced Bradley, winning by over a million and a half votes. Alan Cranston won re-election to a fourth term in the U.S. Senate, defeating Republican Rep. Ed Zschau.

Pete Wilson maintained Republican control of the state's chief executive position with his victory over Democrat Dianne Feinstein in November 1990. Wilson's non-ideological, pragmatic philosophy is more in the Warren, not Reagan, mold.

For the first time this century both U.S. Senate seats were up for election in 1992, the extra seat as a result of Pete Wilson's resignation from the Senate, and for the first time in the nation's history two women, Democrats Dianne Feinstein and Barbara Boxer, were elected the the U.S. Senate. 🏛

ABSENTEE BALLOTS

Mail-order voters tip the balance in close elections

By Gale Cook

Reprinted from *California Journal*, February 1991

"The liar's club," California election officials used to call it. Those few determined citizens who completed a daunting affidavit to qualify for an absentee ballot were considered nuisances — cranks who found excuses not to go to the polls like regular folks. That view prevailed through decades when less than 2 percent of the election vote was absentee.

That was then.

This is now: Almost one in five voters routinely uses the absentee ballot. More than 18 percent of the 7.9

Gale Cook, a retired Capitol correspondent for the San Francisco Examiner, *is a freelance writer from El Macero.*

million men and women who voted in the November 6th general election were absentees.

Everyone is doing it. They don't need a reason. They just ask for an absentee ballot — in person, by messenger, by mail, by fax. They do it for convenience, because they're too busy to go to the polling place, or very likely because a political party or election campaign organization sent them an application. It's the new wave.

A water engineer in Davis votes by mail as early as possible (29 days before election day) and thumbtacks on his door the tear-off stub of his ballot, which says: "I have voted. Have you?" This discourages pesky campaign workers and reduces election leaflets left on his porch. When a political campaigner starts a telephone pitch, he cuts in, "I already voted."

The absentee phenomenon reflects an on-the-go society of always-busy, two-worker families. Its members are pressed for time and prefer to make a reasoned decision at the kitchen table about interminable and complex ballots. Wait in line at the polling place? Say, what?

The Democratic-controlled Legislature took the shackles off absentee voting in 1978, reasoning that the party would benefit from eased restrictions. As it turned out, the Republicans were first to cash that blank check. The Democrats seemed to have forgotten that John Kennedy narrowly won California in the polling booths in 1960 but lost the state to Richard Nixon through the absentee ballot count. A fluke, some said.

But 1982 was no fluke. The Republicans quietly sent absentee ballot applications to every GOP household in the state. Los Angeles Mayor Tom Bradley led in the race for governor by 20,000 votes at the polling places but lost to George Deukmejian by the Duke's 113,000-vote victory among absentees.

Democrats have struck back. In 1983 San Francisco Mayor Dianne Feinstein fought off a recall attempt by persuading 38 percent of the voters to cast ballots absentee. In a Stanislaus County special congressional election in 1989, Democrat Gary Condit defeated Republican Clare Berryhill through an absentee drive. Forty percent of Condit's 50,000 votes were absentee. Democrat Sal Cannella then used the same technique to win the Assembly seat vacated by Condit. In San Diego, Democrat Lucy Killea defeated Republican Carol Bentley in a Senate race in which absentees settled the matter.

Impressed, Stanislaus County supervisors briefly considered asking Senator Dan McCorquodale, a San Jose Democrat, to carry a bill to authorize all-mail elections, but backed off in the face of strong conservative opposition.

Election officials point out that under the present system each absentee vote costs counties about $10 compared to $2 per vote at the polls. On the other hand, all-mail elections — with a few polling places kept open for last minute voters — could cut election costs in half.

"I think that would be real difficult to get that to go over with the public at this point," said Karen Matthews, Stanislaus' registrar of voters.

California's absentee ballot system, one of the most liberal in the nation, was twice challenged in court last year by losers. San Francisco District Attorney Arlo Smith, the Democratic candidate for attorney general, led Republican Dan Lungren by about 30,000 votes in the election night count. Absentee voters, chiefly in Orange County, eventually gave the race to Lungren by about the same figure.

Smith challenged all 1.4 million absentee ballots on the grounds that, while election officials checked signatures on ballot envelopes, 37 counties didn't do so on ballot applications. The judge turned Smith down, saying that even if technical violations occurred, Section 1001 of the elections code required that the law "shall be liberally construed in favor of the absent voter."

In Berkeley, where Mayor Loni Hancock had a 77-vote lead in a runoff, her challenger asked the court to order counting of 386 mail ballots not received by the close of election day. The judge declined, pointing out that the law does not make an exception for delays in the mail, postmark notwithstanding.

Absentee voting is not new in the United States. In 1656 the Massachusetts Colony proclaimed that voters — in other words, male citizens — "shall have liberty ... to send their voices by proxy." The New Plymouth Colony ordained in 1672 that proxy votes would be permitted for reasons of "age, disability of body, urgent occupation and other inconveniences that do accrue sundry of the freemen." Proxy voting was a necessity in those days because in-person balloting would require the virtual evacuation of able-bodied men from the farmlands and frontiers.

The California Legislature first tried to permit absentee voting during the Civil War. In 1863 it passed two acts that would have allowed Union soldiers to vote away from home. A court held these statutes unconstitutional because the soldiers were not residing in their home counties.

In 1914, with the Great War beginning, a constitutional amendment was placed on the California ballot to allow absent voting by citizens who were 10 miles or more from home on election day. It was defeated 390,330 to 244,855.

Further attempts failed at the polls in 1918 and 1920, but in 1922, with opposition dwindling, voters narrowly approved absentee balloting, 352,822 to 340,257. Its use was rigidly defined, but the process was liberalized over the years.

The word "fraud" has been bandied about increasingly with the rise in absentee voting. Nobody can prove it, but the suspicion is there, bolstered by massive absentee-ballot drives in political campaigns. The state Republican Party mailed absentee-voter applications to four million GOP households last year.

Ernest Hawkins, Sacramento County registrar, cites the potential for creating a roll of "ghost voters." These ghostly intruders would be fake names enrolled by postcard registration, which is legal in California; the ghosts then would become undetectable absentee-ballot voters in future elections.

Privately, a Senate staffer said, "No [district attorney] in his right mind would waste his time on election violations with drug dealing and heavy crime around."

All this has caused harrumphing in newspaper editorial columns. Nobody comes right out against voting by mail, but the editorial board consensus is that the Legislature, which

> **"We've found that it's an excellent way to mobilize the base and get votes in from people who for whatever reason might not make it to the polls on election day."**
> **— Dan Schnur**

opened this tap, should — well — take a good hard look at it.

The *San Francisco Chronicle* declared recently: "It is important to encourage increased voter participation in a time of disappointing turnout, but the Legislature should explore the possibility of doing so without permitting the use of absentee voting as just another example of political guile."

Noting the potential for fraud, *The Sacramento Bee* warned that "there is a growing chance that public trust in the electoral process will be undermined," and called for "a top to bottom review of the absentee voter system."

While acknowledging that voting by mail one day may be the way to go, the *San Francisco Examiner* said: "But the Legislature needs to tighten the rules under which absentee ballots are distributed. Campaign workers should not be permitted to apply for ballots in behalf of voters. There is too much potential for abuse. Whether in person or by mail, voting needs to be honest." Most election officials say talk of fraud is blown out of proportion. One who makes no bones about it is Conny McCormack, San Diego county registrar and member of a task force created by Secretary of State March Fong Eu to study absentee issues.

"Most [fraud talk] is paranoia," she said. "I think it's totally not there. I think this is not a problem. We do not see fraud. I don't say we don't see mistakes. We just haven't seen fraud. I think it is just one of those red herrings for campaigns to talk about, especially losing campaigns."

Nevertheless, opponents raise a legitimate issue in charging that county registrars fail to check voter signatures on absentee-ballot applications as well as on the ballot envelopes when the vote comes in.

The language is murky indeed in Section 1007 of the Elections Code. It says the signature on an absentee-ballot envelope "must" be compared with that on the original voter registration. As for signatures and addresses on absentee-ballot applications, those merely "should" be checked.

It would be "hideously redundant and expensive ... to check the signature at the application stage," McCormack said.

Thirty-six other county registrars agree, and Melissa Warren, Secretary Eu's media director, said: "Our contention is that this is optional, that those counties [which skip the application screening do so] in the interest of getting the ballot to the voter."

Although Republicans traditionally oppose liberalizing the voting process, the party takes an understandably serene view of the absentee-ballot system in California.

"We're real supportive of an aggressive absentee program," said Dan Schnur, a former GOP spokesman who now serves as Governor Pete Wilson's deputy director for communications and public affairs. "We've found that it's an excellent way to mobilize the base and get votes in from people who, for whatever reason, might not make it to the polls on election day."

The opportunity for fraud does exist, Schnur said, and the party would view an all-mail ballot as extreme. The important thing is to give the voters an option, he said.

"Our concern is mobilizing the vote. Whatever the guidelines are, we'll follow to the nth degree. You set the rules and we'll play by them," said Schnur.

Senate Democratic leader David Roberti said he is worried that the proliferation of absentee voting may cause "an abridgement of privacy" through applications "filled out by persons other than the applicant."

Former Governor Jerry Brown, state chairman of the Democratic Party, said the absentee ballot increases voter turnout but is hugely expensive as a campaign tool and tends to be used largely by upper-income and therefore more conservative voters. Most of the voters it rallies always vote anyway, he said, and new voters in that group may be only about 20 percent of the total.

"It's like a new high-tech weapon, which really doesn't give you any advantage because the other side has the same thing," he said. "I don't know about fraud, but it is an enormous expense, just another layer of campaign spending making politics more dependent on special interests money."

Brown said the increase in the use of absentee ballots obscures the fact that voter turn-out is declining. The 58.6 percent turnout of registered voters November 6th was the lowest of this century — and only 41 percent of the state's 19.2 million population. "Fewer people [175,183 fewer] voted in 1990 than voted in 1982 when I ran against Wilson," Brown said.

"The absentee ballot is good, but the state must [go to] automatic registration. With the absentee ballot should be state enrollment of all citizens over 18 to vote. The registration thing was invented to depress turnout. Before 1900 most states didn't have registration," said the former governor. "And we have to get some public financing in the form of discounted mailings and free television time."

Ever the visionary, Brown added: "I am in favor of voting by computer or by telephone ultimately. That's where we're going. We can't live in the horse-and-buggy age forever."

In any case, the absentee ballot is going to be reexamined in the Legislature this year and next. Hearings are being scheduled in the Assembly and Senate elections committees, and lawmakers are mulling over election-law bills to introduce.

"There will be a spate of legislation," one staffer predicted. Said another, "People just don't want to wait 40 days to find out the results of an election."

Caren Daniels-Meade, chief of the Secretary of State's elections division and chair of the absentee-ballot task force, said measures will be taken to standardize and clarify the handling, verifying and counting of absentee ballots.

All this might raise a smile from a one-time state senator and attorney general — the late Robert Kenny. In 1939 he introduced SB14 calling for all-mail elections. It was ignored. 🏛

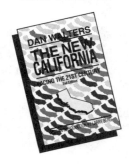

Who are they?

Check out their political agenda: public financing of campaigns; pro-choice on abortion; universal health care; radical cuts in military spending; bans on clear-cutting forests, pesticides, animal-growth hormones and offshore oil drilling; basic rights for housing, child care, education and employment for all — regardless of race or sexual orientation.

The Democratic Party, you say?

Try again — Democrats hate them.

Surely not the Republican Party?

No, but Republicans — including some of the more conservative — like them and wish them well.

Confused?

They're — ta da — the Green Party. And as of January 1, 1992, they'd registered 96,354 Californians under their banner — substantially more than the 80,000 signatures needed to qualify us for a spot on the 1992 ballot. Come June, they'll be right in there with Democrats and Republicans and Libertarians and American Independents and Peace and Freedomites.

The Green Party is the first new party to qualify for the California ballot since the Libertarians appeared in 1980. Two other so-called "third parties" were founded in 1968: the American Independent Party and the Peace and Freedom Party.

The decision to launch the Greens' voter-registration effort in California grew out of a dream by activist Kent Smith, a Sacramentan who has since become state party chairman. According to Smith, he dreamed about a lush soccer field where two teams held sway. Smith and his fellow activists were relegated to the bleachers. "I saw us sitting on our hands while Republicans and Democrats dominated the field of public policy," Smith said. Motivated by that dream, Smith helped organize a meeting of 60 like-minded activists from around the state. And from that meeting, held in Sacramento in February 1990, came the decision to launch a statewide voter-registration drive meant to put Greens on the 1992 ballot.

The California Green Party is part of an national environmental movement known as the Green Committees of Correspondence, a nationwide organization formed in 1984 and made up of more than 200 local groups across the United States. About 40 of these groups are in California. It is modeled after European Green parties, which were successful in gaining significant political influence in the 1980s, especially in Germany and in Sweden. In the United States, the Greens already have made it on the ballot in Alaska and expect to make it soon in Hawaii, Arizona and Pennsylvania.

To qualify in California, the Green Party mounted a volunteer-driven voter-registration drive that featured tables at supermarkets, college campuses and civic and shopping centers across the state. According to Smith, the Green Party drive was unique because it was a statewide effort that was localized, featuring separate drives in what Smith called "10 autonomous regions."

"It was truly a grass-roots effort," said Smith. "We are not a centralized party. We are decentralized, and we think our success proved that you can succeed statewide using autonomous regions." As to be expected, the party was most

New party has Democrats seeing ... Green

By Christian Ettinger and A.G. Block

Reprinted from *California Journal*, February 1992

Christian Ettinger is a California Journal *intern. A.G. Block is managing editor of the* Journal.

suc-cessful recruiting members from the nine-county San Francisco Bay area, which supplied more than 51,000 signatures.

The Greens' recruiting drive snared a cross section of Californians. According to Hank Chapot, a Bay Area Green activist, 20 to 30 percent of those who signed up for the Green Party were previously unregistered, 50 percent were former Democrats and 20 to 30 percent were former Republicans. There were even a few Peace and Freedom converts.

The Greens registration drive may have come along at just the right time because of widespread dissatisfaction with business-as-usual politics. "You just have to spend one weekend registering voters to realize how great a demand exists for an alternative party," said Shelley Martin, director of the San Francisco registration drive.

The state Democratic Party is less than enthusiastic about the Greens' presence on the ballot because it sees it as a threat to the Democratic voter base. Bob Mulholland, the Democrats' political director, warned that the Greens actually could harm the environmental movement by weakening Democrats and giving Republicans and their business allies more room to exploit the environment. According to the *San Francisco Bay Guardian*, Mulholland was so concerned about the Green threat that he tried to squelch the Greens' voter-registration effort by offering jobs to Green organizers Joe Louis Hoffman and Hank Chapot and by sending out a mailing to Green Party members urging them to abandon the party before the December 31st deadline.

"All other parties are enemies. The Greens are no different than the Republicans," Mulholland told the *Guardian*. "If the Greens became a party in California, Republicans will be the happiest party in the state."

Mulholland denied the charges levelled at him in the *Guardian*. "The story ... was one of the most inaccurate stories I've ever read. I never made an offer to Hank Chapot, but he did come up and visit me here in Sacramento and jokingly said to me, 'Make me an offer.' As for Joe Louis Hoffman, he had previously worked in a Democratic voter-registration drive. I called to rehire him and had no idea he worked for the Greens. Finally, I am considering a mailing to Green voters in retaliation for a Green mailing to 18,000 registered Democratic voters signed by David Brower with a voter registration card enclosed."

Mulholland also responded in a letter to the *Bay Guardian*. "While the Democrats backed crucial state initiatives like Big Green and Prop 65, the toxics initiative, where were the Greens?" he asked. "The Republicans opposed us, and the Greens were meeting in a mountain retreat, I guess."

The *Guardian* article also inferred that California Republicans offered to fund the Green Party's ballot drive — a charge hotly denied by the Greens. "We have no money," said Chapot. "This is a volunteer effort."

Party chairman Kent Smith, however, did acknowledge that an anonymous "angel" stepped forward with a $20,000 donation to fund a last-minute paid, signature-gathering drive that added 10,000 members to the Greens' roll. Smith said the extra signatures turned out not to be necessary.

Not all Democratic Party officials agreed with Mulholland's gloom-and-doom assessment. Said one party spokesperson: "A Green Party could strengthen the hand of our progressive wing. We'll be able to say, 'Look, if we don't address environmental issues, we'll lose people to the Greens.'"

According to Smith, party activists are split on how best to proceed with involvement in the upcoming election. Some want no Green candidates because they feel the party isn't ready to compete and could emerge from the elections with the image of a loser. Others feel the party ought to gain electoral experience by running candidates everywhere. Still others want the party to run candidates in selected legislative and congressional races where Green candidates could help decide an election by playing the role of spoiler. Ultimately, Smith said, the decision on whom to run, and where to run, will be left to local Green regions.

Chapot indicated that if the Greens plunge into the 1992 elections with slates of candidates, the bulk of the party's focus will be on city council and supervisorial races.

Party officials want it understood that the Greens are not just an environmental party but are concerned with linking environmental issues with economic, peace and social-justice issues. Many of the party's leaders are veteran activists from single-issue causes like pro-choice, disarmament and toxics.

The Greens have a nine-point platform that goes beyond caring for the environment. Among other things, it stresses electoral reform and campaign funding limits, public financing of campaigns, term limits and more statewide initiatives. It also calls for universal health care; rights to housing, child care, education and employment to all regardless of race or sexual orientation; steep cuts in military spending; and a multi-cultural curriculum in education. The Greens also are pro-choice on abortion. And, of course, they are staunch for laws that protect the environment: elimination of unnecessary packaging and a recyling model that provides a market for recycled products; bans on pesticides, animal growth hormones, clear-cutting of forest lands and offshore oil drilling.

The Green platform is similar to that of the Peace and Freedom Party, but P&F officials do not feel threatened. Maureen Smith, a representative from the Peace and Freedom Party, does not feel as though the Greens invaded their electoral territory. "The Greens will be a positive addition to the ballot," she said, adding that there is a large enough pool of dissatisfied and unregistered voters to keep both parties on the ballot. "There is room enough for both parties to thrive," Smith said. "What we need is an ambitious voter registration to bring all these non-voters into the political process."

Next on their agenda, according to Hank Chapot, is the goal of a half-million registered voters statewide. "We're nowhere near our saturation level," he said. "Even in the Bay Area, where we've gotten most of our voters, there remain many more potential Greens."

"We're determined to do things differently," said party chairman Smith, referring to the Greens' emphasis on local autonomy and grass-roots organizing. "That's more important that winning elections."

Even if a Green candidate never wins an election in California, Smith considers the party successful because California is a bellweather state. He predicts that, because of his party's success in California, Greens will be on the ballot in a majority of states by 1994. The Greens' success in California has, in Smith's words, "galvanized voter registration efforts all over the country. They tell us, 'If you can do it in California, we can do it anywhere.'" 🏛

Did 1992 herald the dawn of Latino political power?

illustration by Lynwood Montgomery

Reprinted from *California Journal*, January 1993

By Dale Maharidge

One August day in the summer of 1970, 12-year-old Martha Escutia was mowing her grandfather's lawn in East Los Angeles. A few blocks away, cops were tear-gassing 5000 Chicano protesters. Escutia's parents kept close reins on their daughter to keep her away from trouble. Anything could happen, as journalist Ruben Salazar was to learn that day. After covering the riot, he stopped for a beer in a Whittier Avenue bar when it was unexpectedly surrounded by Los Angeles sheriff's deputies. A tear-gas shell blasted point-blank into the bar hit Salazar, killing him. Although Salazar's death was ruled accidental, it smacked of an execution and made him into a martyr. Salazar is no Latino version of Malcolm X, but as a *Los Angeles Times* columnist and *KMEX-TV* news director, he was *the* voice for area Latinos. He pushed hard on stories such as Latinos dying with mysterious regularity while in sheriff's custody.

At that time, Latinos had no real voice in California state politics: None were in the state Senate (the last time a seat was held was in 1913); in the Assembly, there was just one Latino.

The Latino community made political gains over the next two decades, but the 1992 elections heralded the biggest change in this century — a record 10 Latinos in the Legislature. All the action was in the Assembly, where there was an increase from four to seven seats (three more are in the Senate), with six going to freshmen — including the now-

Dale Maharidge is a Pulitzer Prize-winning author and former reporter for The Sacramento Bee. *He currently teaches journalism at Stanford.*

grown Martha Escutia.

Escutia and the others are heirs to a legacy with its roots in a Chicano movement that took Latinos from the streets to the halls of power in numbers not seen in modern times. Many are unaware that in 1847, the military governor of California had seven advisers, four of them Latino. And the new state's Legislature from 1849 through 1864 had mostly proportional Latino representation, before the long drought began.

"This is the starting point for the next major shift for Latino power in California," said Richard Martinez, executive director for the Southwest Voter Registration Education Project.

Reapportionment by the state Supreme Court that created heavily Latino districts is certainly a factor but does not entirely account for the change. The Latino community, the largest minority in the state but long considered politically impotent because of low voter turnout, is no longer dormant.

"The sleeping giant is awakened," said 45th District Assemblyman Richard Polanco, a Democratic incumbent who easily won re-election. "The myth of the past is that, a myth."

Polanco's hyperbole notwithstanding, there are indications of increased Latino involvement — that the giant may be awake. At least, its eyelids are fluttering. Whether or not it is ready to sit up and aggressively flex its muscles remains to be seen.

In the past, Latino voter-turnout rates have been low for a variety of reasons, among them: Major parties have viewed Latinos as invisible and thus have spent little time trying to energize them; unfavorable gerrymandering of districts split the Latino community among various neighboring districts to enhance Democratic chances in those districts; a large chunk of the Latino community was ineligible to vote because they weren't citizens or were underage. Yet Latino activists have argued that if the community had a chance to have a meaningful voice, it would get involved.

The 1992 elections seem to offer some glimpse of the future. In 1988, 7.5 percent of the total votes cast statewide for president came from Latinos. In 1992 it jumped to 10 percent, meaning 1.15 million California Latinos went to the polls, according to Mark DiCamillo, associate director of The Field Poll.

"This was the first little tick upwards that we noted," DiCamillo said of the years of stagnant voting patterns. "The registration efforts are finally starting to pay off. And more Latinos are running in Assembly and congressional races, so this has increased participation."

While notable, Latino increases in the Legislature still are relatively low. In the Assembly, for instance, Latinos represent 8 percent of the legislative body, while they make up 25 percent of the California population.

There seems to be an invisible wall at the Tehachapi Mountains; all Latino legislators are from south of that line. That situation could change this year in the race for an Assembly seat being vacated by Democrat Bruce Bronzan. At

I do not see myself as a Latino politician in that this is the only community I represent. You're only going to be relevant if you address issues of all Californians, not just one community.

— Louis Caldera

least one strong Latino candidate intends to run in the Central Valley district — Bronzan's district director, Cruz Bustamante. And there are plenty of local Latino officeholders in the north poised to run in future legislative races.

One thing is certain: There certainly is no going back to the old days when the only Latino politician of note was Congressman Ed Roybal. A look at Latino politics is a search into the recent and powerless past. Paging through yellowed copies of *La Raza*, a magazine begun in 1970 as a voice of the Chicano movement, one senses there was a never-ending Los Angeles riot in those years. Dozens of pictures show Latinos being held in headlock or pummeled by law officers.

The bloody street battles, if not directly responsible for political gains, at least raised awareness to make change possible. The first Latino legislators who came into office, however, were held up as oddities, the subject of much scrutiny, not only among the press but among their fellow lawmakers. There also was a focus on Latino infighting that reached legendary proportions during a bitter 1982 state Senate primary between incumbent Democrat Alex Garcia and Assemblyman Art Torres. Torres ousted Garcia, but the contest took its toll.

Lately, that infighting has involved Los Angeles County Supervisor Gloria Molina (a former assemblywoman and the first Latina elected to the Legislature in 1982) vs. "the guys" — usually Polanco, Torres, and Los Angeles Councilman Richard Alatorre, also a former assemblyman. This was not a Latina-Latino confrontation, however, since both sides supported both male and female candidates.

The intrigue reached a peak during June's primary when the two camps supported different candidates in most Assembly races in Latino-dominated districts. Molina's camp was the loser, with its only victor being Hilda Solis of the 57th Assembly District in El Monte. The infighting has been the cause of thousands of hours of gossip, has meant the use of untold gallons of printing ink, and has resulted in anger among Latino leaders — not at each other but at the way the factions have been reported.

"No one says the Anglos are going at each other," said Martinez of the Southwest Voter Project. "The Legislature is lousy with factions: Anglos have factions, African-Americans have factions. We're no different than anybody else."

The battle between camps will not continue, according to Solis, who said: "I will be independent. I owe people in my community. I think it's unfortunate that kind of stuff has gone on."

The increased number of Latino legislators also may mean Latinos have reached political maturity, at least in the eyes of other ethnic groups that no longer will have just a handful of Latinos to talk about. And the freshmen differ from past Latino lawmakers. One clear distinction is that four of the six newcomers in the Assembly are women. While this sudden jump might seem surprising, it is a natural and expected evolution, said Richard Santillan, director of the

Ethnic and Woman's Studies Department at California Polytechnic University in Pomona.

"It's not surprising to any of us who study Latin American politics," Santillan said. "Women have always been involved in political organization, around the church, the school. I can trace this back to the 1920s and the 1930s."

In the past, women remained in the background, supporting male candidates, Santillan said, but they are no longer going to stay there. And he added that while many Latino politicians of the recent past came out of labor unions, the newcomers come out of private industry, legal careers, the non-profit sector.

"The qualifications and the demands are now such that the leadership is changing, the background is more educated and worldly," Santillan said.

Those interviewed stressed that they want to use this expertise to solve California's problems.

"We're going to be involved in transportation, technology, economic development," said 46th District Assemblyman Louis Caldera, a Democrat who is a West Point graduate with degrees from Harvard's law and business schools.

They are a diverse group, but among those interviewed, one commonality emerged: All strove to distance themselves from being seen strictly as Latino politicians. Not one ever once used the term "Chicano," preferred by the 1970's activists. The word has fallen out of favor over the more general "Latino." "Chicano" is now relegated to use mostly by academics.

"I do not see myself as a Latino politician in that this is the only community I represent," Caldera said. "You're only going to be relevant if you address issues of all Californians, not just one community."

At least one of the new assemblywomen, Diane Martinez, is even uncomfortable with stories (like this one) that single out Latino gains. Her being Latina is irrelevant and not worthy of mention, she said, and she downplayed it during the race. Martinez resents the seven Latinos in the Assembly being dubbed in some circles as "Los Siete," after their number.

"I think that this is all journalistic racism," said Martinez, another Democrat and the daughter of Congressman Marty Martinez. "You never look at Anglos that way. It sounds like we're running in a gang. It's really very difficult to stomach to be treated as one of 'Los Siete.'"

This distancing from ethnic roots caused a long sigh from longtime Chicano activist Raul Ruiz, who was in front of the bar on August 29, 1970 — the day Ruben Salazar was killed — taking pictures as the sheriff's deputy shot the tear-gas canister without warning. Ruiz, now a professor in the Chicano Studies Department at California State University, Northridge, stopped short of calling the new legislators *vendidos*, or sellouts, but he has been critical.

"They should say 'I am a Chicana,'" Ruiz said. "Often those who struggled the hardest are forgotten, and the little princesses and royal family members get these things bequeathed to them. They don't really deserve to get elected. What you saw elected here was the struggle of two machines, the Alatorre machine and the Molina machine. We do have some representation now. But in many ways the community is worse off. It's democracy, unfortunately sometimes with a small 'd.' The Black community has been served much better by the folks they elected into office. I'm much more im-pressed with the way they serve the community than ours do."

The past does weigh on many of the Latino legislators. For new Assembly members such as Martha Escutia, 35, the past is important — her experience, while perhaps not typical of all 10 Latino lawmakers, illustrates that simple labels do not fit the group. Escutia was the child of "firsts" in her family: first generation to be born in the United States, first to graduate high school, then college. In 1982 she graduated with a law degree from Georgetown. She is an activist, but not along the lines of the Chicanos who were in the streets during her youth.

"I came from a very conservative family," she said. "My family always told me, 'You're not Chicana, you're not Mexican-American. If you have to identify yourself as something, don't hyphenate yourself: You're either American or you're Mexican but you can't be both.' So I never related to the so-called Chicano movement, the *Movimiento*. When I was in college I was frankly too busy trying to do well academically and hold down 45 hours worth of jobs. I just had a different agenda. The agenda was I had to build the foundation in order to be successful, and after that I could become an activist."

Upon graduation, Escutia spent five hard years working in Washington, D.C., for the National Council of La Raza, then heavily involved with the 1986 immigration bill and other issues such as employment and training based on the German model of vocational education — a tough sell in the Reagan years.

Escutia feels the burden of "doing something." When interviewed not long before the November election, she was consumed with worry as she drove around her district that stretches from the southern tip of East Los Angeles through Huntington Park in the south. It is 88 percent Latino, and unlike East Los Angeles, which is now a settled community, has most of the new immigrants. Her district is California in a microcosm: dead factories, a lot of immigrants, gangs, poverty, crowded schools.

Escutia pointed out the poverty in plentiful supply — crowded apartments, jobless men milling about — and asked what she can do to change things in the face of monumental problems and a lack of money.

"I don't know how I'm going to do it. My ass is on the line," Escutia said as she gripped the wheel. But Escutia, an intense and passionate woman, is going to try. She feels that one way is to forge coalitions to work together instead of stupidly splitting over lines drawn by camps and ethnic groups.

"LA is on the verge of balkanization," Escutia said. "We're dividing into hostile groups. I resent that a lot of our traditional allies [are] fighting against each other. It's almost like piranhas."

The Black caucus is prepared to work with the Latinos, according to Democratic Assemblyman Curtis Tucker Jr. of Inglewood. The two ethnic groups will hold together now more than ever before, he feels, at least better than the Anglo West Los Angeles liberal legislators and their northern counterparts.

"We all want the same things," said Tucker. "We all want better education, affordable housing, health care, economic development. The difference in wants between the African-American community and the Latino community don't exist." 🏛

DIRECT DEMOCRACY

In California government the people have three tools that make them very powerful participants in the decision-making process. The initiative, referendum and recall were instituted by Governor Hiram Johnson and the progressives in part to break the hold of the railroad interests on state government in the early 1900's. With all three of the direct democracy devices, a simple majority of those voting determines whether the proposal passes.

• *Initiative.* The initiative gives the people the right to place local or state measures on the ballot if they obtain the required number of signatures. It has also been used by governors, legislators and special-interest groups to get what they want after the Legislature has rejected or been unable to meet their demands. To qualify for the ballot, a statewide constitutional initiative requires signatures equal to eight percent of the vote cast in the last gubernatorial election; initiative statutes require five percent.

After the 1990 gubernatorial election the number of signatures required is:

Constitutional initiative - 615,957
Statutory initiative - 384,973

Today, a powerful and sophisticated initiative industry has developed: signature-gathering firms, pollsters, political lawyers, and campaign management firms specializing in the qualifying and passing of ballot measures.

• *Referendum.* This is a procedure that can be used by the public, if they can gather sufficient signatures, to block a state statute or local ordinance pending a popular vote on the issue. It is not used often, but the threat of a referendum occasionally has the effect of blocking enactment of legislation. This procedure cannot be used to stop urgency bills, and for this reason emergency measures require a two-thirds vote rather than a simple majority in the Legislature. The referendum procedure was used successfully at the state-wide level to place four measures the Peripheral Canal and three reapportionment plans — on the ballot in June 1982.

The number of signatures required is the same as for a statutory initiative.

• *Recall.* The third of the Johnson direct-government reforms establishes a petition procedure for placing on the ballot the question of removing any elected official or officials from office. Recall elections are common in local government but have never been employed successfully at the state level in California.

California's system of direct democracy does not stop here. The Constitution and local-government charters can be amended only by a vote of the electorate. Neither the state nor any local governmental agency may incur a general-obligation debt without prior approval of the electorate (although revenue bonds can be sold without such approval). At the state level, a simple majority vote is sufficient to approve bond measures for such purposes as higher-education construction, park acquisition and development, the Cal-Vet farm and home program, and water-pollution plants. But at the local level, all bond proposals — even school bonds — require a two-thirds majority.

In recent years, the potency of direct democracy in California has grown. This power was demonstrated by the far-reaching tax revolt, which started with Proposition 13, the Jarvis-Gann property-tax initiative in 1978. This was followed with the "Spirit of 13" spending-limitation measure enacted in 1979, a successful Jarvis-sponsored income-tax indexing proposal in June of 1982, the successful Gann Legislative Reform Initiative of June 1984 and a number of other Proposition 13 follow-up measures thereafter. Proposition 140 imposes term limits on California elected officials, plus it mandates a 38 percent cut in the legislature's budget. Proposition 164 imposes term limits on our U.S. Senators and Members of the House of Representatives. The number of measures qualifying for the ballot shows no sign of abating in the near future.

With these tools, there is hardly any aspect of state government that cannot be controlled by the people. 🏛

LAWMAKERS AND INITIATIVES

Are ballot measures the magic ride to success?

Reprinted from *California Journal*, September 1988

By Charles Bell and Charles Price

Early this century, California Progressives, led by their fiery governor, Hiram Johnson, put into state codes and the state Constitution a monumental package of critically important political reforms. More than 75 years later, these reforms continue to shape and influence contemporary political life in this state. Among the many reforms promoted by California Progressives, none, perhaps, has had more significance and long-lasting impact than the initiative. The initiative grants the public the right to propose and enact laws and constitutional amendments through a petition and election process. Progressives wanted the public to have the last word in case legislators were corrupt, overly partisan, or dominated by special interests.

Since its adoption in 1911, hundreds of initiatives have been filed by private citizens or interest-group leaders seeking change from outside the governmental system. Elected officials, on the other hand, have invariably pursued change from within the system in the Legislature and executive. As Kelly Kimball, president of the signature-gathering firm of Kimball Management, noted, "Prior to the 1970s most California legislators were only vaguely aware of the initiative process and how it worked. They rarely thought about it as a potential option for them to use in pursuing their legislative objectives." Indeed, many state legislators would have viewed initiative authoring by members as a breech of legislative protocol.

Over the last two decades, however, this attitude has changed dramatically. Today, state officeholders and ex-officeholders are major participants in initiative authoring. Since 1970, approximately 15 percent of all initiatives filed have been by officeholder-proponents. Indeed, over the last several years (since 1983) about 22 percent of initiatives introduced yearly have been authored by current or ex-officeholders.

Charles G. Bell is professor emeritus, California State University, Fullerton, and visiting professor, UC Davis. Charles M. Price is a professor at California State University, Chico.

Moreover, elected officials are more successful at getting their measures on the ballot and have been proponents of more than one-third of all the initiatives qualifying for the ballot over the last two decades. As Mike Arno of American Petition Consultants (another professional petition company operating in California) states, "Officeholders are more realistic [than private citizens] about the difficulties of qualifying initiatives. They understand the need to raise money, and they know how to raise it. Also they don't wait too late before planning their signature drive."

However, once initiatives have qualified for the ballot, private citizens' initiatives win voter approval (39 percent) at about the same rate as do officeholders' initiatives (41 percent).

The trend toward officeholder initiative lawmaking, coupled with private-citizen proponents hiring specialized petition attorneys skilled in formulating law (see "The petition business," *CJ*, July 1985) to draft their measures, means that a substantial number of direct-democracy propositions qualifying for the ballot lately have been written by the "experts." Thus, the criticism by some Democratic legislative leaders that initiatives are largely the product of cranks, crackpots and curmudgeons — people abysmally ignorant of the complexities of lawmaking — does not accurately reflect a substantial portion of recent initiatives qualifying for the ballot.

Why are so many state elected officials mounting initiative drives these days? First, the increase in initiatives written by officeholders began at about the same time as the overall resurgence in initiative filing. Thus, only 17 initiatives were filed in the 1950s, only 44 in the 1960s, but 180 were filed in the 1970s and some 204 thus far have been filed in the 1980s. Many of the same reasons cited by direct-democracy experts to explain the increase in initiative filing generally are also factors encouraging elected officals to try to bypass their colleagues as well. Factors such as lack of confidence or trust in state governmental institutions, popularity of particular initiatives (such as the Jarvis-Gann Proposition 13 of June 1978), and the ease in hiring experts from professional-petition firms to secure at least some, if not all, of the signatures needed might presumably encourage officeholders to try the initiative process.

Second, for conservative Republicans in the Legislature, the initiative (and referendum as well) has provided a tantalyzing way to tweak Democratic leadership noses while at the same time achieving policy objectives.

"We've seen increased partisianship and bitterness in the Legislature, which has led to deadlock and frustration with the process," noted Republican Assemblyman Ross Johnson of Fullerton, author of several ballot measures, including the successful June 1988 campaign-reform initiative, Proposition 73.

Tony Quinn, a Republican reapportionment expert, argues that prior to Proposition 13 of 1978, Republican officeholders tended to shy away from authoring initiatives because the process was viewed as an anti-establishment device. "Proposition 13 suggested the initiative could be used to make policy from the right," Quinn stated.

The success of that initiative wasn't lost on conservative Republicans. "Jarvis and Gann became folk heroes," noted Johnson, "Now, politically ambitious people see the initiative as a [public relations] vehicle."

Since 1978 Republican incumbents have proposed twice as many initiatives as have Democrats. Republican Johnson, author of five separate initiatives in the 1980s (two were on the same ballot), has become the Legislature's equivalent of Paul Gann. Other conservatives in Republican legislative ranks, such as H.L. Richardson, former state Senator John Briggs, John Doolittle, Richard Mountjoy, Don Rogers, Doris Allen, Tom McClintock and Congressman William Dannemeyer, also have been active authoring initiatives.

Indeed, one recently filed criminal-law initiative has no less than nine co-proponents, including three Republican state legislators — Ed Davis, Ed Royce and Johnson — plus six other Republican local activists. While most of these conservative Republican initiatives deal with substantive policy issues, a number have been directed against the Democratic legislative leadership. Former Sonoma GOP Assemblyman Don Sebastiani's reapportionment initiative, Governor George Deukmejian's initiative to have retired appellate judges do reapportioning, and Assembly Minority Leader Pat Nolan's sponsorship of the Gann legislative-reform initiative are examples.

Third, on the Democratic side, a few moderate or liberal legislators have also on occasion proposed initiatives, such as Assemblyman Lloyd Connelly of Sacramento, Senator Joseph Montoya of Whittier, Assemblyman Richard Polanco of Los Angeles and former Santa Clara County state Senator Arlen Gregorio. Some Democrats have turned to authoring initiatives because Republican Governor Deukmejian has vetoed or threatened to veto their bills. However, if Republicans should capture control of the Legislature in the 1990s, it is highly likely that many more Democratic legislators will begin to energetically exercise this option, while Republicans may prefer to work within the legislative arena.

Fourth, some of the Legislature's leading mavericks, such as Democratic Senator Alan Robbins from the San Fernando Valley, independent Senator Quentin Kopp of San Francisco, or former Republican Assemblyman Sebastiani are also found in the initiative-author ranks perhaps because they see themselves as outsiders in the legislative system. Indeed, one might also anticipate initiative salvos from the Assembly's "Gang of Five" in the months ahead.

Fifth, politicians anticipating runs for higher political office sometimes author initiatives to help generate publicity for their campaigns. For example, former Secretary of State Jerry Brown championed Proposition 9, the 1974 Political Reform initiative, in his quest to become governor, and Briggs authored death penalty and homosexual teacher initiatives in his bid to become governor. Clearly, it was the fame Paul Gann derived from authoring so many controversial initiatives that made him a formidable candidate when he sought the Republican nomination for U.S. Senate in 1980. There also appear to be definite political overtones to Superintendent of Public Instruction Bill Honig's full-page advertisements in several of the state's major newspapers endorsing the insurance industry's no-fault car insurance initiative.

Sometimes, however, a politician-sponsored initiative may actually hinder its sponsor's bid for higher office, or the bid for higher office may doom the initiative. According to Caren Daniels-Meade, press secretary to Secretary of State March Fong Eu, Eu's "Dimes Against Crimes" initiative was hurt by her U.S. Senate candidacy. "On occasion people were reluctant to support Eu's initiative because it might be viewed as if they were endorsing her candidacy in the U.S. Senate race."

Even though Eu eventually suspended her U.S. Senate campaign in order to get potential financial supporters off the hook, it was too late. And, without financing, Eu could not afford to hire a professional petition company to collect the necessary signatures.

Finally, a prime advantage of initiative-passed law over legislative-passed law is that the former locks in change. Laws passed by the Legislature are constantly being amended; initiatives once approved are far more difficult and cumbersome to amend, and this asset is well understood by elected officeholders.

Ever since the initiative was incorporated into the California Constitution, there has been substantial overlap between the legislative and initiative lawmaking processes. Over the years, legislators have sometimes been threatened by potential proponents that if they didn't pass a particular bill, an initiative would be filed which would be far more extreme than the legislative measure.

In turn, legislators have sometimes passed constitutional amendments to go on the ballot as alternatives to previously qualfied initiatives. Currently, for example, the Senate Insurance, Claims and Corporations Committee reluctantly approved a constitutional amendment by Democratic State Senator Herschel Rosenthal to establish an insurance commission which would be charged with approving or disapproving insurance-rate hikes. Though several committee members felt Rosenthal's constitutional amendment was flawed, they voted for it to head off eight separate insurance-reform initiatives seeking qualification on the November 1988 ballot (five eventually qualified). Ross Johnson, for one, believes the initiative process gives him added clout. "The initiative does work as a lever on pending legislation. I have demonstrated that I can get an initiative on the ballot," Johnson said.

On some initiative efforts, officeholders are heavily involved in the drafting and also are publicly identified as sponsors of the measure. But for a variety of strategic or political reasons, they are not listed as proponents. For example, Governor Ronald Reagan (tax-reform initiative of 1973), Governor Jerry Brown (Political Reform Act of 1974), or conservative Republican Assembly Minority Leader Pat Nolan (Legislative Reform Initiative of 1983), while prominently involved with sponsoring these measures, were not technically their proponents.

Also, because of their political prominence, office-holders are frequently asked to write the pro or con arguments in the secretary of state's official *Voters' Handbook*. In addition, incumbents sometimes tape television or radio spots to extol or attack a proposed initiative. For example, Governor George Deukmejian urged voters to support his initiative to establish an independent reapportionment commission, and Attorney General John Van de Kamp said voters should vote "no" on the "deep pocket" insurance-reform initiative (Proposition 51, June 1986).

What are the implications in having officeholders author so many initiatives? In theory, the initiative was supposed to be a sort of last-resort option for private citizens to propose new laws or constitutional change, thus bypassing a recalcitrant Legislature. In reality, the problems such as heightened partisanship, special-interest influence, political opportunism, public distrust and friction between the governor and the Legislature have contributed to a shift to initiative lawmaking and away from legislative lawmaking. Until these problems are resolved, it is likely that there will continue to be a significant number of incumbent initiatives. And, the more officeholder initiatives on the ballot, the likelier the frustration in an increasingly irrelevant Legislature. Indeed, one of the initiative's sharpest critics, Assembly Speaker Willie Brown, commented recently that he wished a particular initiative had been launched in the Legislature.

"I'd prefer to see it debated, the dialogue elevated, in the halls of the Legislature," he said, admitting, "Politicians are usually not risk-takers and that even if similar legislation were introduced, it would be a slow, ponderous procedure."

There were six initiatives on the June 1988 ballot, an unprecedented number for a primary election. There are 12 on the ballot in November. And the state may be fast approaching (if it hasn't already) the point of no return in terms of voter overload. Extensive initiative lawmaking by politicians clearly indicates a troubled state Legislature. 🏛

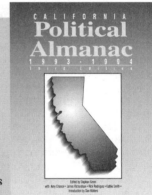
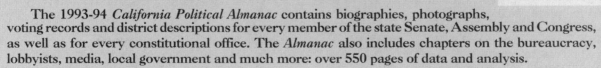

Initiatives: too much of a good thing?

By Charles Price and Robert Waste

Reprinted from *California Journal*, March 1991

The old bromide about the weather — "Everybody talks about it, but nobody can do anything about it " — has also been true of California's initiative process. For years, critics of this direct-democracy technique have complained about the problems and abuses inherent in the process. But thus far, efforts to substantially reform the initiative have failed.

Politicians have usually been wary of proposing major changes because the initiative has always been popular with the public. As a result, initiative procedures today are approximately the same as in 1911 when the process was first adopted, even though the state's population-growth now mandates the collection of hundreds of thousands of signatures (5 percent of the vote cast for governor in the most recent election for statute initiatives; 8 percent for constitutional amendments) before a measure can qualify for the ballot.

Despite the hurdle, the initiative process is more popular than ever. Modern campaign methods, including computerized mailing of petitions and paid circulators, have encouraged those who can raise the necessary $1 million or so to bypass the Legislature and go directly to the public.

However, there are indications that the public, deluged by ballot measures in the past few years and faced with an increasingly complex array of issues to discern, now may be willing to accept some changes in the initiative procedure. Some legislators have quickly stepped in and are proposing major alterations in the state's process of direct democracy.

The initiative was promoted by reformist Progressives early this century as a last resort technique for the public. If the Legislature were corrupt or controlled by special interests or party bosses, voters using the initiative process could adopt laws and constitutional amendments without the Legislature or governor. During the early decades of this century the initiative was employed frequently. But by the 1940s, during World War II and in the years immediately afterwards, initiative activity declined sharply. However, in the 1970s-80s and in 1990, there has been a tremendous resurgence of initiative activity.

The number of initiatives filed has nearly doubled each decade from the 1950s to the 1990s. More initiatives have been filed in a single year, 1990, than in entire decades from the 1910s through the 1960s. Intriguingly, while only about one-third of initiatives were approved by voters up to 1979, in the 1980s nearly one-half were approved.

There are a number of reasons for this surge in initiative activity, including the development of a professional petition industry — petition companies, initiative attorneys

Charles Price and Robert Waste are political science professors at California State University, Chico.

and campaign consultants whose livelihood depends on a continual fresh flow of initiatives; a public angered by legislative inaction and political scandals; the success of some efforts, such as property tax-slashing Proposition 13; the growth of single-issue politics; increasing use of counter-initiatives (groups threatened by an initiative place an alternative initiative on the ballot); and a growing trend towards elected officials authoring initiatives as part of their campaign strategy in running for statewide office.

When only a few initiatives qualified for each ballot, the process was grudgingly accepted by state officeholders. However, adoption by voters of the Political Reform Act (Proposition 9, 1974), the Gann state spending limitation initiative (Proposition 4, 1979) and, perhaps most important, the term-limit initiative (Proposition 140, 1990) which may cut legislative careers to a maximum of six or eight years, angered a great many public officials. Through the mid-1980s, however, polls showed the public overwhelmingly supported the initiative process. Mervin Field reported in 1979 that 83 percent of the California public thought the initiative was a "good thing," while only 5 percent thought it was a "bad thing." The public seemed to agree with the theme of the "yes on Proposition 13" campaign — the initiative was a good way to "teach the politicians a lesson." Therefore, attempts by various, mainly Democratic California legislators to reform the initiative (usually proposals to make it harder to qualify initiatives — e.g., raising the filing fee or requiring that petitions be signed in a certain number of counties) were regularly defeated. In addition, in *Meyer v. Grant* (1988), a federal court ruled that states could not prohibit paid signature soliciting — a favorite target of initiative critics.

However, the convergence of a number of factors indicates that for the first time this century the time may be ripe for significant initiative reform. Why is this so?

• First, clearly, the public was very unhappy with the number of voting decisions facing them in the 1988 and 1990 elections, caused mostly by the number of initiatives on those ballots. An all-time record number of initiatives, 18, qualified in 1988; two years later, this figure was equaled when another 18 initiatives appeared on the primary and general election ballots. However, ballot length was not simply a result of too many initiatives. As Bill Arno of American Petition Consultants noted, "Actually, there were more legislatively referred measures than initiatives on the 1990 ballot, and if the Legislature had been doing its job there wouldn't have been so many initiatives."

• Second, the public was upset with the length, complexity and confusing nature of many of the 1988-90 initiatives. The 1990 Ballot "Pamphlet" and supplement came to 221 pages of complicated legal argument. In this vein, pollster Mervin Field reports that public support for the initia-

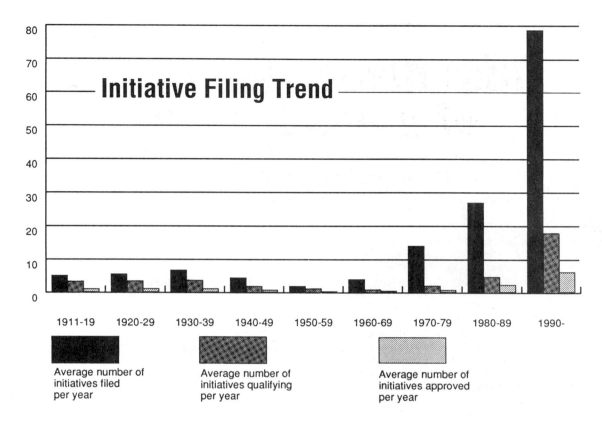

Initiative Filing Trend

80
70
60
50
40
30
20
10
0

1911-19   1920-29   1930-39   1940-49   1950-59   1960-69   1970-79   1980-89   1990-

Average number of initiatives filed per year

Average number of initiatives qualifying per year

Average number of initiatives approved per year

tive process has declined 16 percent since 1979. Currently, "only" 66 percent of Californians view the initiative as a "good thing."

• Third, initiatives have not been faring well in the courts lately, and this adds to public frustration over the process. Thus, just a few weeks prior to the November 1990 general election, Propositions 73 and 68 — two campaign-finance initiatives approved by voters in June 1988 — were declared unconstitutional. In addition, Proposition 103 — the auto-insurance rate-reduction initiative from November 1988 — has been so enmeshed in legal challenge that public hopes for quick insurance-rate reductions went unrealized. However, two years after the adoption of Proposition 103, State Farm Mutual in December 1990 under a plan approved by the Department of Insurance will substantially lower its rates for "good" drivers. The courts even stepped in and voided Proposition 105, an omnibus "consumer protection" measure that required disclosure of everything from insurance policies to household toxics on the previously uninvoked restriction in the state constitution requiring initiatives to deal only with a "single subject."

• Fourth, there is growing public resentment over the devious, deceptive and expensive media campaigns by initiative sponsors and opponents. In addition, the new trend evidenced in 1988 and 1990 revolves around electoral competition between environmental or political reform groups and their corporate opponents. If the former gets its initiative on the ballot, the latter will hire a petition firm to put forward its own counter-initiative on the same topic. There were four sets of counter-initiatives on the November 1990 ballot, while in the November 1988 election, five separate initiatives focused on auto insurance. Counter-initiatives have one main objective: confuse voters. As Kelly Kimball of Kimball Petition Management stated, "I'm disgusted with groups that put measures on the ballot to confuse and deceive voters, and who prefer that their counter-measures don't pass. Enough's enough."

• Fifth, many officeholders were bitter that a majority of the electorate would support the term-limits initiative, which not only cut short legislative careers but imposed a nearly 40 percent reduction in the Legislature's own budget, causing widespread layoffs among legislative staff and did away with legislators' retirement benefits.

• Sixth, there was a massive "no" vote registered against most of the initiatives (10 of 13) and most of the other propositions and bond measures on the 1990 general-election ballot. As Democratic Senator Milton Marks of San Francisco noted, "The outcome of the November [1990] election was a clear indictment of the initiative process."

• Seventh, many of the major players in the state's initiative industry — for example, Ted Costa, executive director of the Paul Gann People's Advocate, and petition circulators Kelly Kimball and Bill Arno — now believe the process needs to be reformed.

• Eighth, rejection by voters of Proposition 137 (November 1990), an initiative designed to make it more difficult to reform the initiative process (it would have required a majority vote of the public before any change could be made in the initiative process) and recent Mervin Field polls indicate growing public support for initiative reform. Joel Fox, executive director of the Howard Jarvis Taxpayers Association, said, "The public's rejection of Proposition 137 caught me by complete surprise."

Thus, there is at least some support among officeholders from both parties and the public that special interests have tended to monopolize and control the initiative process and that reforms are needed. What is not clear is the shape reforms should take. Should reform aim at discouraging use of the initiative, as some legislators want? Or, should reform aim at restoring the process to the people? And, as both Kelly Kimball and Bill Arno noted, if the Legislature adopts measures to make it more difficult to qualify initiatives, this will benefit their petition-for-hire companies because they will be the only ones around who have the expertise to collect the hundreds of thousands of signatures needed.

Among the various reforms being proposed by elected officials, Senate Republican leader Ken Maddy of Fresno has proposed a constitutional amendment to more clearly express the single-subject initiative requirement — "An initiative measure embracing more than one subject may not be submitted to the electors or have any effect."

Should Maddy's bill pass, initiative provisions would have to be reasonably germane and interdependent with other provisions of the measure. Of course, what is "reasonably germane" is subjective and subject to court interpretation. Ironically, the Maddy bill passed the Senate but failed in the Assembly last year when it was *joined* to a proposal to move the presidential primary ahead.

Opponents of "Big Green" (Proposition 128, November 1990) argued that it failed to meet the single-subject requirement, but since it was not approved the question is moot. Proposition 105, the court-voided consumer-information initiative approved by voters in November 1988, had five separate sub-categories — toxic substances, fraudulent health insurance, nursing homes, initiative campaign funds and stock-selling corporations conducting business in South Africa. Although the court acted in this case, it historically has been loathe to do so. The last time the court struck down an initiative for violation of this principle was 1948. Unquestionably, lengthy propositions with many subsections complicate decision making for voters but agreeing on what is "reasonably germane" is not easy.

Among other legislators who favor reform of the initiative, Assembly Speaker Willie Brown of San Francisco favors having initiatives voted upon only during general elections, not during primaries, because of the poor turnout in these June contests. (Of course, the percentage voting in the general election these days is not very high either). If this were implemented, it would mean the general-election ballot would be substantially longer and might further voter frustration.

Senate President pro Tempore David Roberti has suggested that initiative petitions should have to obtain signatures in a certain number of counties. Democratic Senator Gary Hart of Santa Barbara is contemplating legislation to prohibit bond issue initiatives. Independent Senator Quentin Kopp unsuccessfully authored a bill in the last legislative session aimed at discouraging initiative proponents from building support for their measures by offering groups who joined the coalition funding from the measure for their pet projects. Of course, log-rolling is a long-time practice in the Legislature. Proponents raise money for their initiatives, then pay themselves substantial consulting fees from the campaign treasury. Marks stated, "We need to somehow take away the profit involved with initiatives."

Republican Assemblyman Stan Statham is the author of AB 3148 which was signed into law by former Governor George Deukmejian. This law requires a notice that the petition may be circulated by either a volunteer or by a paid signature gatherer, and the public has the right to inquire as to the circulator's status.

Statham noted that, "Not a soul at the Capitol doesn't know that the initiative process is warped and out of control." Democratic Assemblywoman Jackie Speier of South San Francisco proposed in a bill last session that the Secretary of State do a legal analysis of a proposed initiative to ensure the proposal was in proper legal form. At present, initiative proponents can seek aid from the Legislative Counsel in drafting their proposals. But, according to Ted

Costa, when he asked the Counsel's office for help in drafting an initiative, he was told that because of the passage of Proposition 13 and state spending limits, the counsel's office did not have sufficient staff to help him. Not surprisingly, initiative advocates worry that if the secretary of state's office or attorney general's office did a precirculation legal review of the initiative it could be partisanly-inspired because these are elected partisan officeholders.

UC Berkeley Professor Eugene Lee argues that "consideration be given to a minimum threshold in turnout, say, 50 percent of registered voters, as a condition of passage to ensure the 'people's voice' is heard." However, initiative advocates might well ask, why should this only affect initiatives? Shouldn't candidates be under the same proviso? And, since turnout in primaries is usually below 50 percent of those registered, how would we nominate our candidates? Lee also proposes that the Legislature and governor be allowed to amend and repeal statutory initiatives after a specified time and that the constitutional amendment initiative signature threshold percentage be raised from 8 percent to 10 percent.

Yet, while the time may be ripe for reform, there may be good reason to proceed slowly. There are always unanticipated consequences of any reform. In one sense, the abuse of the initiative process in 1990 was dealt with by the voters. They massively voted "no" — not a bad strategy considering all of the confusing proposals on that ballot. And, because they voted down so many measures, won't those who buy their way onto the ballot be less enthused about trying this tactic in 1992? Also, the election of Governor Pete Wilson may encourage environmentalists to pursue the legislative path once again. As Gerry Meral, executive director of the Planning and Conservation League, said, "The PCL had to go the initiative route because of Governor Deukmejian's obstinance. We may not have to do this with Wilson."

It should be emphasized: An overwhelming majority of the public (66 percent according to Field) still supports the initiative. Efforts to discourage initiative use according to Ted Costa might lead to a coalescence of interest groups ranging from Tom Hayden's Campaign California, Harvey Rosenfield's Voter Revolt, Ralph Nader's Public Interest Research Group, environmental groups such as the Planning and Conservation League and Sierra Club on the left of the political spectrum to Ted Costa's People's Advocate, Richard Gann, Ralph Morrell, and Joel Fox of the Howard Jarvis Taxpayers Association on the right. These disparate groups might be willing to pull together to thwart legislative attempts to discourage initiative use.

Finally, are initiatives the central problem facing California government? Democratic Assemblyman Ted Lempert of San Mateo, a member of the Assembly Elections and Reapportionment Committee, doesn't think so. "Initiatives are usually a yes or no on a basic idea. That's good and has its place but the Legislature is where the real work is done. That's where we have the hearings and make detailed policy. That's the level at which we have to get the people interested again. That's the real reform of all of this."

And echoing these sentiments, Martin Smith, political editor of *The Sacramento Bee* observes, "The problem is not so much initiative procedure as an underlying problem of government not working. Maybe something can be done at the margins with initiatives but the real disease is government that doesn't work and hasn't worked in at least 16 years of not very dynamic leadership." ▲

Signing for fun and profit:

the business of gathering petition signatures

illustration by Wendy Rudick Shaul

BY CHARLES M. PRICE

Reprinted from *California Journal,* November 1992

Well, they're back. After a brief respite from initiative politicking in the June 1992 primary, a small platoon of signature-qualified propositions invaded the November 1992 ballot (Propositions 161-167). While dozens of initiatives were launched by hopeful proponents, only these seven made it.

Why did they succeed where all others failed? Professional petitioning.

The seven were all jockeyed to ballot status through the efforts of California's only two "out-in-the-streets" signature companies: Kimball Petition Management of Los Angeles, and American Petition Consultants of Sacramento.

All it would have taken for the failed initiatives to qualify was money. Had their backers the money to hire Kimball or American, their proposals, too, would have reached the ballot. Qualifying initiatives using only volunteer activists and shoestring budgets is very difficult. Qualifying an initiative is expensive and lately seems to be the exclusive province of the well-heeled. For instance, according to the secretary of state, 80 percent of the money raised to qualify November's seven initiatives came from contributors giving more than $10,000. (Not only that, the first petition measure to qualify for the June *1994* primary ballot — the school choice or 'voucher' initiative — also used paid petitioners.)

The qualified initiatives and their professional petitioners are:

Charles Price is a professor of political science at California State University, Chico, and a frequent contributor to California Journal.

Prop	Title	Signature Company
161	Assisted Death	American
162	Public Employees Retirement	Kimball
163	Snack Tax Elimination	Kimball
164	Congressional Term Limits	American
165	Budget and Welfare Reform	American
166	Health Care	Kimball
167	State Taxes	Kimball
???	School Choice	American

Brothers Kelly and Fred Kimball Jr. are managing partners of Kimball Petition Managment, which their father founded in the 1960s. While Fred Senior was an arch-conservative who helped qualify many right-wing issues for the ballot (for example, Proposition 6 of 1978, which would have allowed school districts to fire homosexual teachers), Kelly and Fred Junior have shifted their company's ideological focus to more mainstream and even some liberal issues. Thus, in November 1992 the Kimballs worked on petition campaigns for Democratic-leaning interest groups such as state employees, the Tax Reform Association and the California Teachers Association. Since the late 1960s, Kimball has qualified dozens of petitions for state and local ballots.

American Petition Consultants also is the province of two brothers — Mike and Bill Arno. Mike is president, while Bill serves as director of operations. Their firm has qualified mainly Republican-conservative issues over the last decade, however American did qualify the liberal-leaning "Death with Dignity," for this fall. Said Mike Arno, "Philosophically,

I'm opposed to [Proposition 161], but it's a social issue that ought to be decided by the people, not the Legislature."

Despite the fact that they are competitors, competition in the signature-gathering business is not quite like competition in the personal computer business. And the links between the Kimballs and Arnos go back many years. Mike Arno's wife grew up as a neighbor of the Kimballs in Southern California. She persuaded Fred Senior to give Mike his first chance in petitioning as a crew chief for Kimball in the early 1980s, and he learned the business well. Over the years on a few occasions, when deadlines are imminent, Kimball and American have sometimes subcontracted with each other for a certain number of signatures. They've been friendly competitors — until this year.

Clearly, Kimball and American dominate initiative qualifying these days. Between 1982 and 1992 nearly 75 percent (48 of 65) of all of the initiatives on the California ballot have qualified through the efforts of one or the other of these two companies. Once hired, they virtually guarantee their clients' ballot status (each has a nearly a 100 percent success rate). Both firms also earn considerable sums qualifying initiatives in states like Oregon, Nevada, Washington, Michigan, Ohio, Oklahoma and Colorado. And, since the collapse of Communist rule in Eastern Europe, each firm has done consulting work in the newly emerging democracies there. Indeed, another Arno brother, Peter, runs their company's St. Petersburg/Moscow operations, and plans are afoot to establish a new office in Minsk.

Paid petitioning wasn't always needed to get a measure on the ballot in California. In the early years, after the initiative was placed into the state Constitution by reformist Progressives in the 1910s, qualifying could be handled by volunteers because proponents had 150 days to collect fewer than 50,000 signatures — a number based on a certain percentage of the total vote cast for governor at the most recent election (5 percent for a statute; 8 percent for a constitutional amendment).

But as California's population increased massively during the Great Depression and after World War II, collecting and processing the hundreds of thousands of signatures needed within the 150-day circulation period became a logistical nightmare — hence, professional petitioning. And since 1990, when the Colorado Supreme Court refused to review a lower court decision that states could not ban paid petitioning because it limited free speech, paid petitioners have truly come into their own.

Through the early 1980s the paid petitioning process went something like this:

• Kimball or American is contacted by an initiative proponent, and the two sides would settle on a price for collecting a specified number of paid signatures — 100,000 or 200,000, for example, with the remainder usually gathered by volunteers.

• The measure then is submitted to the attorney general's office, which assigns it an official title and summary and looks over the text to make sure it's above board and legal. The attorney general laterals it to the secretary of state's office, which assigns circulation and signature-verification deadlines.

• Thousands of copies of the petition are printed and

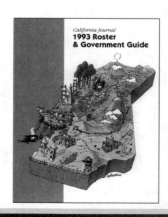

sent to the Kimball or American crew chiefs around the state.

• Crew chiefs hire reliable solicitors by contacting people from previous campaigns and by advertising for new ones in the classifieds.

• Crew chiefs brief their solicitors on a summary of the main arguments for the initiative and point them toward the best places to find signatures — for instance, shopping centers or where people are waiting in line.

• Crew chiefs also teach solicitors how to persuade a reluctant prospect by saying, "This doesn't mean you agree. It's just to get the measure on the ballot so the people will have a chance to vote on it."

• Solicitors turn in their signatures, receiving 25 to 35 cents per name. Crew chiefs earn 5 to 10 cents for all signatures collected in the city or area.

• Finally, proponents turn their accumulated signatures in to local county clerks for validation and tabulation.

Although paid petitioning in the 1990s follows a similar procedure, there are some interesting new twists in the business.

• **Independent subcontractors:** In the old days, American and Kimball had loyal crew chiefs who worked only for one or the other. But no more. As American's Mike Arno noted, "Today, our crew chiefs [located in most of the state's larger cities] are independent subcontractors. In the old days, we hired a lot of 'mom and pop' operators; for example, housewives who ran petition drives out of their homes. These days our subcontractors all have their own businesses. We try to buy the best contractors available.

"Sometimes, they're ones that have done a lot of Kimball work. These people are free agents and negotiate their best price. So, too, the solicitors are independents. A crew chief says, 'I'll give you 35 cents per signature,' and a solicitor says, 'I want 45 cents, or I won't do it.'"

Moreover, Kelly Kimball noted, "If you're slow in getting signatures, you've got to raise the price for the solicitors. It's a stock market out there. Some circulators will delay turning in their signatures on one of the petitions they're carrying, assuming the price will go up. It never goes down. We raise the price [per signature], and suddenly thousands of signatures come in. They bought low and sold high."

• **Multiple petitions:** To make money in petitioning these days, Kimball and American must have packages of three or four or five initiatives — not merely a single initiative — to entice the best petition subcontractors to work for them. George Gorton, Governor Pete Wilson's campaign manager who was spearheading the governor's budget-welfare reform initiative qualifying effort in 1991, failed in his attempts to negotiate contracts with petition subcontractors. The subcontractors want packages of initiatives because the more petitions, the more money and the better enticement for successful solicitors. In addition, subcontractors prefer to do business with known quantities. Wilson's forces eventually sought out Arno to collect the signatures for what has become Proposition 165.

Said Kimball: "There is no limit to what these people [solicitors] can carry."

Arno, in a similar vein, added: "The most petitions I've ever seen one solicitor handle was 13. He had every initiative ... on an ironing board. People would walk along the board, and he'd say, 'Are you for this one? ... Sign here. This one? ... Sign here. This one?' Some solicitors can make as much as

$30 or $40 dollars an hour. Several have made $50,000-$60,000 in a five-month period."

• **Initiative awareness:** Before 1978 and Howard Jarvis' property-tax slashing Proposition 13, the initiative process was not well understood by most interest groups. To attain policy objectives, these groups preferred to concentrate on lobbying and providing campaign contributions to candidates. In the 1990s, however, those same interest groups (and elected officials, as well) are keenly aware of the initiative option, and of the ability of Kimball and American to collect hundreds of thousands of signatures. Consequently, the petition business has picked up steam. In addition, American and Kimball advertise in various political journals (including *California Journal*) to publicize their accomplishments.

However, neither Kimball nor Arno say they try to talk people into filing an initiative — usually. Kimball acknowledged that he put together the Lottery initiative as a pro-active effort. "We were looking for something we could make money on, and somebody who would fund it," Kimball said. "But, there are just too few issues out there like that."

• **Validation:** Another difference between paid petitioning today and yesterday is that the two companies place much more emphasis on collecting *valid* signatures. As Arno explained, "Each of us have computers with lists of all registered voters, and we can do random-sample verifications of signatures brought back by our solicitors. As the petition business has developed, subcontractors don't want to get a reputation for turning in poor work. If they fall below our quality control standard, I can back charge them."

• **Direct mail:** In the early 1980s it looked as if direct-mail companies might supplant street petitioning as the wave of the future. Direct-mail petitioning still is used to supplement some petition drives, but it isn't the main signature source these days. Kimball, more pessimistic than Arno about direct-mail petitioning, warned that direct mail "just flat out doesn't work very well. It worked for Howard Jarvis, and it worked somewhat for [Paul] Gann, but on a limited basis. Many of the people on the Jarvis lists were not young, and some have since died. A direct-mail piece is tremendously expensive. If you don't get a decent contribution return rate, you're spending $10 to $15 to $20 per signature."

• **Motivations of initiative proponents:** On the contemporary scene, initiatives are no longer proposed simply as a last resort by interests failing to get their way in the Legislature. These days some issues are introduced via the initiative process. In addition, some initiatives dealing with the same issue on the same ballot are designed to confuse voters rather than to be approved. Some initiatives are put on the ballot to siphon money from conservative Republicans or liberal Democrats. As a result, the process has become more complicated and Byzantine.

• **The attorney general:** Finally, according to Kimball, the present attorney general, Republican Dan Lungren, has been exceptionally partisan. "The [initiative] summaries his office does contain his political philosophy. They're like campaign literature for the opposition." For instance, attorneys representing proponents of Proposition 167 (the so-called "tax the rich" initiative) had to go to court to get the attorney general's "partisan" summary modified. American's Arno, however, disagrees with Kimball's assessment.

It is still possible for dedicated activists to qualify initiatives in the 1990s, but doing so is a formidable undertaking. Perhaps, the prototype of the idealistic cause/volunteer of petitioning is Ken Masterton of Masterton and Little of Bolinas. Over the last few years, Masterton has directed successful qualification efforts for four different environmental initiatives for the Planning and Conservation League (Proposition 70 of June 1988; Propositions 116 and 117 of June 1990; Proposition 130 of November 1990). In addition, he was successful with Proposition 99 of November 1988 (the tobacco-tax) and Proposition 134 of November 1990 (the alcohol-surtax). While more emphasis is placed on getting volunteer signatures in Masterton's efforts, on most of his petition drives some paid signatures also are collected (indeed, two-thirds of the signatures he collected for Proposition 130 were paid). In addition, to secure his freebie signatures, Masterton must pay coordinators to organize the volunteer solicitors, and it costs thousands just to print all the petitions that will be needed. According to Masterton, the typical volunteer effort to place a statute on the ballot will cost about $250,000 to qualify. Thus, initiative qualifying, even those using mostly volunteer signature collectors, is expensive.

Relations between American and Kimball have cooled recently. The reason: the controversy over the qualification effort for the school-choice, or voucher initiative. Arno was hired by the initiative's proponents to collect the necessary signatures to place the measure on the November 1992 ballot. However, in a unique counter-strategy move, the California Teachers Association hired Kimball as a consultant to work *against* qualification.

"Our strategy in the anti-qualification campaign was to arm the potential signer with the information needed to say 'no,'" said Kimball. "If a well-educated teacher can explain why an initiative is bad to potential signers, this can be very effective. It wouldn't have worked to have our circulators do this. Teachers were ideally suited for it."

Arno, not surprisingly, saw it differently. "On the one hand, you had teachers who saw the choice initiative as a 'life or death' issue and, on the other side, you had people trying to earn money collecting signatures. Many of these people were in agreement with the philosophy of the choice initiative. It's a very frustrating thing to have someone jump in your face when you're trying to collect signatures. We had reports that potential solicitors were offered money not to get signatures, or were threatened if they tried to do so. They used Kelly to locate where all of our people were. If we fail to qualify an initiative, this obviously benefits Kelly."

Arno is convinced that some opponents of the voucher initiative purposely signed the petition more than once to sabotage the effort. "Our duplicate rate was abnormally high," he complained. "Thirty-two people in San Diego County signed the petition more than 10 times and several signed it more than 20 times. This was not an accident." While Arno admits that he ran anti-signing efforts in several local contests, he stated he would not do so again because "it diminishes the process."

Arno blamed the anti-signing campaign and sabotage for the voucher initiative's failure to meet the deadline for the November 1992 ballot. Rather than qualify through a random sampling procedure, every signature had to be verified. The process took so long that the deadline for November 1992 passed, although the measure did qualify for the June 1994 ballot. Both Arno and Kimball viewed this delay as a significant blow to the school-choice initiative. Kimball felt that momentum for the issue will slow, and now the CTA will have two years to raise funds to defeat it. Moreover, teacher campaign money that would have flowed into the effort to defeat the proposal can now be used to help elect allies to the Legislature. According to Arno, "The sad part about all of this is that the CTA basically cheated and got away with it. They know they overstretched the rules."

Both Arno and Kimball are supportive of some reforms to improve the initiative process. Kimball noted, "If it were in my power, I'd really enforce the single-subject rule. I'd also like the system reformed so that voters would be asked a simple question, 'Do you want a state lottery? Yes or no?' And, if a majority of voters say 'yes' then the Legislature would be required to implement the law. We should not have to have voters wade through 20 pages of legal text describing an initiative. People don't have the time or energy for this. My proposal would be a sort of an indirect initiative."

But Arno wants the process to continue. "When I'm invited to speak to college classes," he said, "I always ask this question: 'Were there too many initiatives on the last ballot?' ... 'Which of them would you have like to eliminate from the ballot?' There is always much disagreement on this. 'How many bills were considered by the Legislature last year?' Most think a few hundred. I tell them, 'More than 6000. Can you name five of them?' And, they can't. But they know what the initiatives were. Finally, I ask, 'Who do you trust more — you making the decision or your legislator?' Overwhelmingly, *they* want to make the decision." 🏛

LOCAL GOVERNMENT

One reason why Californians have so many elections and frequently such long ballots is that the state has a complex system of local government. Every citizen in the state probably is a resident of a dozen or more units of local government, among them:

Counties. The state has 58 counties (counting San Francisco), some of which are governed by general state law and others by charters (similar to constitutions) voted by the people.

Cities. Most Californians live in one of the state's 468 cities, but many live in unincorporated areas in which municipal services are provided by the county and special districts. General law cities (384) operate through a structure established by state law. Charter cities have more flexibility in their structure and procedures.

City-county. San Francisco is a combined city and county operating under a charter.

School districts. Public schools from kindergarten through 12th grade are operated by independent districts with directly elected governing boards. There are about 1200 school districts in the state.

Community college districts. Directly elected trustees also run community colleges, which provide freshman and sophomore courses.

Special districts. These can vary from large regional districts such as the Metropolitan Water District in Los Angeles to a local mosquito-abatement district. There are more than 3,000 special districts formed to provide specific services for a defined area. Most directors are elected by the public.

Local Agency Formation Commissions. Each county has a commission that serves as clearinghouse for annexation of territory by a local agency and for formation of new cities.

Regional governments. There are no all-powerful regional governments in California, but there are numerous limited-purpose regional agencies such as the Bay Area Air Pollution Control District, Rapid Transit District and Sewer Service Agency. Efforts have been underway for years to enact a powerful regional government for the San Francisco area. There are several voluntary associations of local governmental agencies designed to help resolve regional problems; these include the Association of Bay Area Governments and the Southern California Association of Governments.

City and county government

Counties are run by boards of supervisors elected by the public, usually by district. In most counties, the board appoints an administrative officer to supervise the details of county government. Counties also have other directly elected officials, such as the district attorney, the sheriff and the assessor.

Cities are operated under a variety of systems. Under one basic arrangement not widely used, the strong-mayor system, the mayor is the chief-administrative officer of the city, and policy is set by the council. The more common system establishes the mayor, who may be elected either by the people or by the council, as the ceremonial chief of the city and puts the administration of municipal affairs under the control of a powerful city manager or administrator. The council has the power to appoint and remove the manager. Under this council-manager form of government, the council is supposed to be limited to the setting of policy, but there have been a few cases in which a mayor, by virtue of a strong personality, had been able to run the city government, relegating the manager to the role of errand boy.

More frequently, however, the manager, by virtue of the fact that he is a full-time employee with a large staff, plays a role as large as or even greater than the council in establishing policy.

Special districts are usually administered by a superintendent, general manager or other executive selected by the governing board. 🏛

More cuts, closures on the way?

illustration by Rob Wilson

The state's libraries struggle to do more with less

By Elizabeth Schilling

Reprinted from *California Journal*, January 1993

Libraries, along with other public services, have taken their share of budget hits in recent years. Rural residents, such as those in Mendocino and Shasta counties, endure periodic closures of their entire library systems. Urban and suburban residents everywhere are losing their neighborhood libraries. And while traditional library users are seeing the doors close, many librarians feel that even more alarming is the fact that most immigrant groups have never developed the habit of going through library doors in the first place.

"Libraries are the underpinning of our democracy," contends state Librarian Gary Strong. "They help with the business of life-long learning and getting along in our society. Yet libraries are taken for granted and viewed as non-essential when it comes to cutting a budget."

Libraries have had to do more with less, but not less of everything: A truckload of social problems has been dumped on the doorsteps of the state's 700 libraries, according to Anne Turner, director of libraries for the Santa Cruz city-county system.

"In many cases, libraries are left to be the only symbol of government presence in a neighborhood," Turner explains. "If there is no shelter, we must take care of the homeless. If an after-school program is cut, we become the drop-off point. As schools eliminate their libraries, we pick up the slack — and we do it all without being given another penny."

As a result, libraries have exercised astonishing creativ-

Elizabeth Schilling is a freelance writer from Santa Cruz.

ity to do more with less. Volunteers record oral histories; computers help readers reserve books; and in Los Angeles County, a compact disc connected to a fax machine delivers magazine pages to far-flung library branches.

"People's information needs are no longer confined to just books," adds Turner. "Based on people's requests, we provide everything from gardening videos to college catalogs. Others need employment seminars or large-print books. As society changes, our definition of information needs to get broader."

And exactly which language should be used to respond to requests is another dilemma before librarians. In addition to English, large cities such as San Francisco have substantial collections in Spanish and Chinese.

"Serving multiple cultures is a growing challenge," says Neel Parikh, chief of branches with the San Francisco Public Library, which has had its budget cut $1 million annually since 1988. "We experiment in downgrading our service. We've cut hours, hired para-professionals and converted full library branches to 'reading centers.'"

Meanwhile in Berkeley, where residents twice approved a tax to fund their libraries, the current best-sellers had better be ready and waiting when readers come looking.

"We enjoy the best support of any library in California. This is both a blessing and a curse," says Regina Minudri, director of library services for the city of Berkeley. "Because citizens are aware of how much they pay, they like to see where their money goes."

Berkeley residents know exactly what they contribute to their library because an assessment appears on their tax bill. Voters first approved an assessment in 1980 when Proposition 13 cutbacks began to erode their library services. To avoid a direct property tax, the city council devised a building assessment: For each square foot of structure, residences were assessed three-and-a-half cents and commercial buildings six-and-a-half cents. The referendum was approved with a 70 percent majority.

Despite the community's good intentions, the tax proved insufficient by the second year. "We miscalculated," says Minudri. "No one had ever done anything like this before and we had no idea so much of the city was of tax-exempt status."

Luckily, voters were understanding. In 1988 they approved an increase to seven cents for residences and 11 cents for commercial structures.

Minudri, past president of the American Library Association, predicts such assessments will be the future lifeblood for many libraries. Besides directing her system, Minudri currently is consulting with 12 jurisdictions around the state where library referendums are being considered.

"I recommend the assessment only under certain circumstances. It worked in Berkeley because it's a wonderful, crazy community packed into 10-square miles," says Minudri. "A community must be well-educated and have a high density where no one is far from a library. That profile does not fit very many places."

> "How many libraries do we have? Now, that's a tricky question. This morning we had 92; effective Monday we'll have 83."
>
> — Sandra Reuben, Head Librarian
> Los Angeles County

Santa Paula, Merced, Davis and San Francisco are some of the cities that have approved assessments for either library construction or operation.

Perhaps paying for a library makes people appreciate it. In Berkeley, for instance, usage is up 43 percent since 1980, Minudri brags. The national book circulation per capita is four; in Berkeley it's 12.

All of California's 168 library jurisdictions have been on their own to endure cuts as they feel the impact of Propostion 13. Unlike other public services, libraries are unable to impose or increase user fees. Libraries are even worse off than health services, says Turner, since such agencies can still find federal grants. Overall, the state contributes only 2 percent to local libraries. Most systems are still reeling from last year's cuts under AB 8, which took $1.3 billion from local governments and special districts and shifted it to schools.

The 1993-94 budget year threatens deeper cuts. Conservative estimates predict that libraries throughout the state will loose upwards of $60 million. To make matters worse, Governor Pete Wilson is expected to fully eliminate the Public Library Foundation, which last year gave libraries a token $10 million.

Librarians are adapting by working more closely together. They're advising each other on technology and sharing regional resources. A soon-to-be-released report produced by a statewide coaliton of librarians and the California Library Association will offer an agenda on how to cope with what looks to be a dismal future. The coalition, which has met for four years, has studied everything from the use of school libraries to the formation of special districts.

Sandra Reuben, head librarian in Los Angeles County, says that last year, $10.2 million was slashed from her budget of $70 million. Of the 88 cities that make up the Los Angeles area, her system serves the 55 unincorporated ones. The massive area includes all socio-economic groups and more than 50 minority populations. The Los Angeles riots closed 34 of the system's branches for a week or more.

"How many libraries do we have? Now, that's a tricky question," Reuben said during a November interview immediately following a public hearing on library services. "This morning we had 92; effective Monday we'll have 83."

The closures were the results of county general fund deficits for 1992. "Now I'll hold my breath for another six months until we see how bad 1993 will be," says Reuben. "Proposals already on the table say our library funds could be cut by 50 percent."

Library users will have to "get beyond dependence on a building," adds Reuben. "We could never do without buildings, but technology can add to this traditional need. The upcoming switch will be similar to banks going to ATMs. It will take the public a while to adjust, but then they may find that they like their new libraries even better."

Before getting to this brighter day, however, California libraries and their advocates must brace themselves for many cold dawns. 🏛

illustration by Christopher Van Overloop

OUT OF THE SANDBOX

Sacramento city politics may go big-time

By Ed Goldman

Reprinted from *California Journal*, May 1993

"SANDBOX POLITICS" is how one local newspaper used to characterize municipal doings in Sacramento. For, despite the town's status-by-proxy (or, more appropriately, by-proximity) as California's capital city, journalists found it difficult to take seriously the day-to-day decision-making of its part-time City Council.

That may be about to change. With the election last year of Joe Serna Jr. as mayor, and the recent retirement of City Manager Walter Slipe after a remarkable (for this line of work) 17-year tenure, a movement is afoot to create a full-time mayor/council government. Under one system being discussed, the manager — the professional administrator appointed by the City Council and currently given near-autonomous authority to fill roughly 200 Civil Service-exempt positions — would cede a good deal of real and perceived policy-making power to the mayor. If that happens, some observers are saying, it may embolden other mid-size California cities to take a second look at their own versions of the traditional council/manager form of government.

Which is not to say that the proposed switch, which would require that Sacramento's more than 70-year-old city charter be amended, is anywhere near a done deal. Local voters have resisted at least three different attempts to alter the charter to even grant councilmembers a pay raise. They earn

$20 per meeting; given the expansive nature of most of their meetings — particularly if land-use, high-rise development or neighborhood issues dominate that week's agenda — this works out to about 25 cents an hour. Factor in the average 25 hours per week that members spend in their city hall offices responding to constituent calls, letters and drop-ins, and you have a pretty strong argument for the IRS to consider the holding of this elective office as a charitable contribution.

"This city has grown so much in the past 20 years alone," Slipe said a few days before his retirement, "that it's ridiculous to expect people with full-time jobs to also handle full-time

Ed Goldman, who once worked for Walter Slipe, now is a Sacramento-based writer and consultant.

city council responsibilities." Slipe supports the notion of a full-time mayor and City Council; he is less sanguine about the notion of a "strong" mayor system, wherein the elected official also serves as the chief executive, relegating the manager's role to that of fiscal policeman.

"The council/manager form of government came into being as a direct response to corruption and cronyism" in the latter part of the 19th and early part of the 20th centuries, Slipe said. "When people tell me they support a strong mayor/weak manager form of government, I say, 'So you're in favor of the way [the late Mayor] Richard [J.] Daley ran Chicago? Swell!' Then they say, 'Wait a minute. Is that what would happen?'"

Mayor Serna dismisses Slipe's fears.

"There's just as much opportunity for corruption and cronyism under a strong manager/weak mayor [system] as there is the other way around," Serna argues. "But if he wants to say that, then I'll just point to the way Robert Moses ran the city of New York, practically unchallenged, and say, 'Oh, this is what you want? A professional bureaucrat making all of the decisions for the elected officials?'" (Moses, the late public works director of New York, was the subject of Robert Caro's Pulitzer Prize-winning biography, "The Power Broker.")

Serna and Slipe both think that Richard Daley and Robert Moses achieved great things for their respective cities. In fact, says Slipe's successor, William Edgar, "I really don't think that Joe and Walt are far apart on this issue. It's just a matter of degrees." Of what? "Power."

Serna is a long-time political science professor at California State University, Sacramento, a frequent campaign manager for Democratic candidates, and a highly respected community activist who won the mayor's seat outright during the primaries. "I think that if people elect you to represent them, and then you're not given the power to hire and fire people, to make essential decisions or to implement policies, it shows a certain disrespect for the voters," he insists. "It says, 'You're not smart enough to choose your own representatives. We'd better bring in some professionals to get the job done.'

"The way things are right now, elected officials in this city have all the accountability but none of the responsibility. If we had a situation like Los Angeles had, where the mayor [Tom Bradley] clearly wanted to fire his police chief [Darryl Gates], well, hell, I couldn't fire the chief. Only the city manager, who hired him, could. But who do you think the voters are going to blame when they go to the polls? The city manager? Of course not. They'll blame their mayor."

Serna says the ballot box is the built-in control mechanism in a full-time mayor/council form of government. "The voters tell you just what they think every four years," he says, "and they can throw you out."

Told this, Sacramento's new city manager Edgar smiles. "That may be true," he says, "but as city manager, I run for re-election every Tuesday night [when the council meets]."

In Sacramento, as in most similarly crafted city governments, it's one vote easier to seat a city manager than to sack one: five of the nine council-members must approve the hiring; six the firing. Which means, Serna says, "To suggest that a city manager doesn't

Walter Slipe by Rich Pedroncelli

constantly count votes is naive at best. A good city manager is a good politician. He has to be. The city manager has to make sure he never gets six people mad at him at the same time. In all the years I've been on the City Council [since 1981], there's never been a vote of no-confidence in Walter Slipe. He's done a magnificent job here, there's no doubt of it. But he's also been intensely political."

As might be expected in a city that plays host to the Legislature, local elected officials tend to monitor what's going on under the Capitol dome a few short blocks from city hall, not unlike the way a younger sibling might look up to his or her elder. "People who come on this council are, generally, pretty ambitious," Serna says. "They care about their community but they also know they have a pretty good base of operations for [launching a career in] politics."

In fact, since the late 1970s Sacramento councilmembers have run successfully for Congress (Democrat Robert Matsui); Assembly (Democrats Phil Isenberg and Lloyd Connelly); and Sacramento County Board of Supervisors (Grantland Johnson).

"One of the problems I have with the city going toward a 'strong' mayor system," Slipe says, "is that some of our [elected] folks look at the Legislature and view that as their model of how good government should operate — with two houses, a speaker, a president pro tem ... the Legislature shouldn't be anybody's model on how to get things

done." Edgar agrees.

In conversations with city government watchers and players, one recurring threshold for determining a municipality's format seemed to be size, although there was an acknowledgment that things are changing, at least attitudinally, in local government.

"I think the threats to the city manager/city council form of government are mostly hitting more urbanized, metropolitan areas," says John Thompson, city manager of Vacaville, a town of more than 80,000 residents midway between Sacramento and San Francisco. "As a city grows, the weight of the [also-growing] bureaucracy is hard for people to handle. They want a mayor and a council-member they can identify with."

A former senior management analyst for Sacramento city hall, Thompson says that city managers are finding they need to be more responsive to citizens — and to neighborhood concerns, in particular. He recalls that at a recent conference of the International City Management Association, "a lot of the older city managers were pretty direct about how they've resisted the idea of doing any consensus-building, among city councilmembers or the public. They feel that their job is to practice good management, not to be political.

"And," Thompson says with a laugh, "if [city managers] ever are identified as political figures, we're doomed!" In the meantime, he adds, a growing trend in city government of all sizes is decentralizing its services to both bring social services into the neighborhoods "and to let people meet some of the people who deliver those services. Not just the elected officials, but the ones who can directly offer assistance. People need to know who's running their government."

Thompson blames the education system for not better preparing students to be informed citizens. "The schools just do a horrible job of explaining how government works," he says. "The only time kids in [Vacaville] find out what form of government their city has is during the hour I speak to the political-science class. ...they really have no idea of how a [smaller] city is run, day-by-day."

One educator who doubts that a trend is afoot to politicize local government operations, and who thinks to do so would be ill-advised, is the University of Southern California's Chester Newland, a highly respected guru of city managers across the country.

"It's not so much a matter of [a city's] size," says Newland, "although that's the usual discussion. For example, Dallas, which is the same size as San Diego, is a council/manager form [of government] and has been for years.... They [councilmembers] don't earn a living being politicians. They work for a living, and then serve as citizens."

"Twice," Newland recalls, "San Diego has considered revising [its form of government]; many, many years ago, and then about three or four years ago, they considered it again. ...[Then-Mayor] Pete Wilson tried to revise the government to a strong mayor/council system while he was there. That failed, you may remember. It is a good example, nonetheless of [showing] when a person has a capable manager, the mayor certainly can exercise very considerable influence and leadership, partly because the mayor doesn't have to do all the day-to-day administration but can really be an aggressive leader."

Responding to Serna's assertion that part-time, "weak" mayors and city councils have all of the accountability but none of the responsibility, Newland says, "Basically, what many of [local elected leaders] would like would be to politicize the system, [and] turn to spoils appointments as a way of having more direct political responsibility. I would say that most people who have watched American politics during this period of growing transactional or 'change' politics [since the 1950s] would probably conclude that the politics is leading us back to a period of rampant spoils."

"The last thing I'd ever do as mayor is hire my political friends for government jobs," Serna says emphatically. "You need the professionals. Under the plan I envision, you'd still have a strong administrator. No one is talking about doing away with city managers, though maybe we wouldn't call them that anymore. We're simply talking about letting people lead who were elected to lead."

Slipe freely admits he wants it both ways. "I strongly believe that for the council/manager form of government to work, you have to have a strong manager and a strong council. It won't work if the manager's strong but the council's weak, or vice versa." He takes out a photocopy of a newspaper article he's hung onto for several weeks — a listing, by New York-based *Financial World* Magazine, of the best-fiscally-

> **B**ut who do you think the voters are going to blame when they go to the polls? The city manager? Of course not. They'll blame their mayor.
> —**Mayor Joe Serna**

managed of the 30 largest U.S. cities. "Of the top four [Dallas, Phoenix, Portland, San Jose], only one doesn't have a council/manager form of government," Slipe says. "That's Portland. And they're considering it."

Of California's 468 cities, more than 50 operate under the mayor/council form of government; the rest under council/manager form. Most of the mayor/council municipalities are small cities (3000 to 20,000 population) — excluding such notable exceptions as Los Angeles, San Diego and San Francisco. At present, no other city besides Sacramento seems poised to restructure its governing system.

Serna maintains that as cities grow, voters will continue to demand knowing who their leaders are, face-to-face. While he has no plans to try introducing a ballot measure to amend the city's charter — "It'd seem just a little self-serving, don't you think?" he asks — his new manager, Edgar, says he anticipates the formation of a citizens' charter commission "in the next year" to weigh the question of a full-time, adequately compensated mayor and council. Yet while Serna says he thinks the commission should evaluate the entire charter "but with absolutely no directions from the elected officials," Edgar says: "No, all they should consider right now is this one question. We don't need to get people bogged down in hundreds of trivial items when this is the first and most important change that needs to be made."

"This push for a full-time mayor and council isn't about power," Serna says. "But I have to tell you, I'm getting real tired of hearing Sacramento referred to as a 'city manager' form of government."

Slipe, too, says he gets upset "when people refer to [Sacramento] as a 'city manager' form of government. It's a council/manager. The council sets the policy and the manager carries it out."

That's a statement that still inspires merriment in Isenberg, the former Sacramento mayor who now serves in the Assembly. At Slipe's retirement dinner, Isenberg — whom Slipe credits with having been a strong mayor (though Isenberg has insisted he accomplished this strictly by allowing others to perceive he had more powers than he did) — said of his longtime friend, "One thing I'll always admire about Walter is that of all the city managers I've heard say, 'The council sets the policy and the manager carries it out,' he's the only one who had the graciousness to at least blush afterward." 🏛

EDUCATION SYSTEM

That "automatic" degree may be a thing of the past

By William Trombley

Reprinted from *California Journal*, December 1991

Crowded classes, canceled classes, higher student fees, faculty layoffs, students who can't get the courses they need to graduate on time, students who can't get classes, period. These stories have rolled in from across the state throughout the fall term on California's public college and university campuses.

While the immediate cause is the state budget crisis that led to spending cuts in both the University of California and California State University systems — and only a small increase for the community colleges — this year, the larger question is whether the state's 31-year-old Master Plan for Higher Education, with its promise of "higher education for all," is still viable.

Many believe it is not.

"There is a fundamental mismatch between resources and enrollments," said William Storey, an assistant director of the California Postsecondary Education Commission (CPEC). "Unless the budget situation improves, those [enrollment] numbers are going to have to come down."

William Trombley is a Capitol reporter for the Los Angeles Times.

Storey referred to recent CPEC projections that enrollment in the University of California will increase from 160,000 to 226,000 by the year 2005, that the California State University will grow from 375,000 to at least 495,000 and that community college enrollment will make an astonishing leap from 1.5 million to 2 million. David Mertes, chancellor of the statewide community college system, said even those numbers are conservative and that he expects enrollment in the two-year colleges to reach 2 million before the end of this decade.

While enrollments soar, state financial support for higher education is declining.

Warren Fox, new director of the Postsecondary Education Commission, which advises the governor and the Legislature on higher-education policy, noted that the percentage of state general fund revenues going to higher education (community colleges, CSU and UC) has dropped from 15.9 percent in 1984-85 to 13.5 percent this year.

That is why many believe a day of reckoning is coming soon for the Master Plan, especially for its promise of a place in a public college or university for every student who could benefit from higher education.

"The structure of the Master Plan will stay," former UC

President Clark Kerr, one of the plan's architects, said, "but the question is whether the state will be able to fulfill the promise of higher education for all who want it."

To Barry Munitz, the new chancellor of the California State University system, the answer clearly is "no," not unless state financial support is increased.

A $60 million reduction in state funding for CSU this year has resulted in laying off or not re-hiring 3000 instructors, eliminating 868 non-faculty positions and wiping out more than 3800 class sections this fall.

If there are more actions like this, Munitz has been telling audiences around the state recently, CSU will not be able to accept the top one-third of California high school graduates — its assignment under the Master Plan.

"We cannot continue to bear a greater and greater burden without fundamentally affecting the quality of the education we deliver," he said.

Although the University of California is not as dependent as CSU on state funding — only about 30 percent of the total UC budget comes from the state, with federal research grants and contracts, student fees and private gifts accounting for most of the rest — the nine-campus UC system still was hit hard by this year's budget cuts. Only by raising student fees a whopping 40 percent and persuading some 4000 faculty and staff members to take early retirement was UC able to avoid canceling class sections this fall.

But outgoing UC President David Gardner said drastic measures such as these cannot be repeated. He warned that UC would begin to deny admission to eligible freshmen (the top 12.5 percent of the high school graduates) if budget cuts continue and if the state is unwilling to pay for a new campus in the San Joaquin Valley.

Some education specialists in Sacramento argue that there is room for UC to expand on several existing campuses, especially at Irvine and Riverside. But Gardner insisted that most UC campuses already are at full capacity or face strong community opposition to expansion.

"We can't build up existing campuses," the UC president said. "Berkeley [current enrollment: 30,500] can't grow to 45,000; Santa Cruz [currently 10,300] can't go to 30,000. Even at levels we think are reasonable, we've had trouble with our communities."

Gardner said he will ask Governor Pete Wilson and the Legislature "if they want to build the tenth campus or not; and, if the answer is 'no,' then I will say, 'All right, under those circumstances, we will not be able to offer a place to all the eligible students seeking admission.'

"'Now you tell us what you are willing to pay for. Should we take just the top 10 percent of high school graduates? Or 8 percent or 7 percent, or what? This is a public policy question that the state of California must answer."

The state's community colleges, which have been the entry point to higher education, as well as to occupational training, for vast numbers of California young people (and some not so young) face even more serious problems than either UC or CSU. If enrollment jumps by half-a-million students over the next decade or so, as is predicted, almost all of the existing 107 two-year colleges will be filled to capacity and 25 to 30 new campuses must be built.

Where will the money come from to build them? Or to operate them, once built? No one knows.

Mertes, the statewide community college chancellor, said there already are about 100,000 "unfunded" students in the system — students whose educations must be financed by local community college districts because state funds have run out. Typically, districts dip into their reserves to pay for unfunded students, which means that a single unexpected problem — a corroded gas line or an air conditioning system that fails — could drive a district into the red.

Mertes also complained of another Master Plan violation. He said many qualified community college graduates are unable to transfer to a four-year campus because there is no room for them.

Although UC and CSU still are able to offer a place on one of their campuses to every qualified transfer student, that place may be so far from the student's home and job as to make attendance impractical. Mertes called on each four-year campus to announce in advance how many transfer spaces would be available each year "so we don't waste our time and our students' time."

Even if problems like a shortage of transfer places could be solved, there is a growing feeling that the Master Plan cannot be patched and stitched together much longer and probably must be abandoned.

State revenues are running below estimates and another multi billion-dollar state deficit in 1992-93 seems probable. Even if the revenue picture were brighter, higher education still would be forced to compete with increasing demands for other state services, like Medi-Cal and elementary and secondary education.

"The future looks bleak," said Carl Rogers, education specialist in the state Department of Finance., "We don't know how we can afford it [i.e., the Master Plan]."

Maureen DiMarco, secretary for child development and education in the Wilson administration, said, "We may not be able to fulfill the Master Plan guarantees, and we ought to confront that very quickly."

Said Harry Wugalter, a member of the Postsecondary Education Commission, "The 'higher education for everybody' idea was developed under a completely different set of circumstances ... it was a great idea but we can't afford it anymore."

Some believe the plan's promise of a college education for all who could benefit from one already has been broken.

"Universal access is shot," said Patrick Callan, former director of the Postsecondary Education Commission and now a higher education consultant. "We're squeezing admissions requirements at UC, pushing more students into CSU, where they can't find classes, so they go to community colleges, where they can't find classes, either."

"In effect," Callan added, "the state is doing away with the Master Plan in a way that leaves no fingerprints."

Kerr said a basic assumption of the Master Plan was that state economic productivity would increase by at least an average 2 percent a year, but it has not done so. Nor, Kerr added, did those who drew up the plan foresee the huge increases that have come about in state spending for health, welfare, elementary and secondary education and prisons.

Between 1988 and 1998, state spending for debt service on state bonds will increase by 16.3 percent, prisons 11.1 percent and Medi-Cal 8.2 percent, but support for UC and Cal State will increase by just 5.6 percent, according to estimates prepared by the Postsecondary Education Commission.

With budgets tightening and the Master Plan in jeopardy, new approaches are being suggested.

"The Master Plan captured the imagination of the country and the world in the 1960s," Callan said, "but now it has become a straightjacket. There's room for a lot of creative thinking about how to move forward."

One of the questions that Callan and others have raised is whether the University of California needs to offer a complete range of graduate and professional programs on all eight general campuses (and on the new San Joaquin Valley campus as well). These critics suggest it would be more cost-effective for the university to concentrate many of its graduate and professional specialties on one or two or three campuses. They also believe the state cannot afford the $1 billion or more that a new, full-blown research campus in the San Joaquin Valley eventually would cost. They suggest that an under-graduate campus, with a few graduate programs, would make more sense.

But Gardner insisted that UC already limits the number of new doctoral and professional programs it initiates, and he suggested that in some fields, the university should be training more professionals, not fewer. For instance, he noted that less than 20 percent of the state's physicians have been trained at the five UC medical schools.

Gardner also defended the plan for the tenth campus, with the same full range of undergraduate, graduate and professional programs found elsewhere in the UC system.

"To assure access and quality, we cannot have what one might call one, two and three-tier institutions in the university," he said. "We know what our institution is and how it works and what it can do. Therefore, when we propose to add a tenth campus, we're not proposing a campus with a different mission."

"This is institutional hubris," Callan responded. "These people are saying, 'We're going to do things the same way we've been doing them for 45 years and, if anybody doesn't like it, that's just too bad.'"

Some have suggested the state could save money by requiring University of California faculty members to do more teaching. Typically, a UC professor teaches one or two classes each quarter or semester, while his counterpart in the California State University system teaches three or four. The rationale for the difference is that UC faculty members are expected to do "cutting edge" research as well. However, many UC officials acknowledge that some professors do little research at all, whether at the cutting edge or not, and don't teach much, either.

Former UC President Kerr said that when he served as chancellor of the Berkeley campus in the 1950s, he sought to determine the average faculty teaching load but soon found that "at the University of California, like other research universities, all of that happens at the level of the academic departments, where there are few policies and nobody keeps records." Kerr concluded that "it would be insanity for any chancellor, or president of the university, to try to do anything about this."

CSU faculty members also will be teaching less as the result of a new agreement between the faculty and the CSU administration requiring efforts to reduce the average teaching load from 12 units per semester to nine over the next three of four years.

Other changes that have been proposed in the state's higher-education arrangements include:

• Increasing the number, and the amount, of "Cal Grants," so that high school graduates may afford to attend one of the state's private colleges or universities instead of a public campus.

• Changing the ratio of upper-division to lower-division students on UC and CSU campuses from 60-40 percent to 75-25 percent so that more freshmen and sophomores could be educated at the less-expensive community colleges.

• Changing state financial incentives so that UC and CSU are rewarded for graduating students, not just for enrolling them. Only 30.5 percent of freshmen who enrolled at a UC campus in the fall of 1982 earned a degree in four years. At CSU, only 27.7 percent of first-time freshmen enrolling in fall 1983 earned a degree in five years.

• Establishing an expansion policy for all three segments — UC, CSU and community colleges — instead of allowing the three segments to lobby the governor and the Legislature for new campuses.

• Using some of the now-sizable pot of UC and CSU student-fee revenue to pay for educational programs, instead of limiting its use to non-academic programs and financial aid.

Mertes startled a meeting of community college chief campus officers a few weeks ago by proposing that the two-year schools dramatize their financial plight by limiting enrollment to students in pre-college or vocational training classes. This would eliminate thousands who come to community colleges to learn English and other basic skills. It would also mean that thousands of disadvantaged students in the state's major cities would be deprived of a chance to prepare for a four-year college or for a vocational career.

"That would be a disaster" in a district like Los Angeles, said Donald Phelps, chancellor of the nine-campus, 122,000-student system. "About 70 percent of our students are minority and many of them lack the basic skills needed for success in four-year colleges. That's why they come to us."

Phelps, who went to college after leaving the Army and began his teaching career at the age of 30, said, "I would have been one of the students eliminated by such a policy." He also warned that limiting access to public higher education just when minorities are beginning to attend in significant numbers would be unwise and dangerous for the state.

State Senator Gary Hart, a Santa Barbara Democrat and chairman of the Senate Education Committee, sounded the same warning. "If we cut back on the 12.5 percent [the UC admissions pool] or the 33 percent [the CSU pool], then all of these issues of affirmative action and ethnic diversity, which are so sensitive, will become even more so," Hart said.

Whatever is done to change the Master Plan for Higher Education will face strong institutional and political opposition. However, unless there is a miraculous change not only in California's year-to-year budgets but also in the state's underlying economic and social conditions, change surely is coming.

Things have gotten so bad, said DiMarco, Governor Wilson's education adviser, that "I have even heard people ask if we can afford to improve K-12 education. If we do, they argue, we'll collapse the whole higher education system because we'll produce more high school graduates and there won't be room on the campuses for them." 🏛

School vouchers

art by Rob Wilson

Will they save or destroy public education?

By Stanley Moss

Reprinted from *California Journal*, June 1992

The initiative that could turn California's public school system topsy-turvy appears headed for a 1993 special election ballot. Long a favorite punching bag wherever people vocalize discontent with "the way things are," the school system could be knocked to its knees when the votes are counted.

Sponsored by a group named ExCel (Excellence through Choice in Education) and backed to the tune of $1.5 million, the initiative is known as Voucher/Choice. Its stated purpose is to improve the quality of education, and it seeks to achieve this by allowing parents, starting with school year 1993-94, to choose the schools — private or public — they think most likely to meet their children's needs. The school of choice would be paid by a voucher

issued to the child by the state. Also, beginning the following year, 1994-95, students enrolled in private schools as of October 1, 1991, would receive similar vouchers.

By pegging the voucher at 50 percent of what public schools receive for each student, based on average daily attendance (ADA), the initiative ensures that the voucher amount keeps up with ADA increases. This year's ADA payment to schools is $5200, making the voucher worth $2600 next year, if voters approve the scheme.

The day the initiative was made public its proponents were singed by angry blasts from all sides. Calculating the devastating cost of vouchers to be paid out of funds earmarked for the state's public schools, educators and others were certain ExCel's real aim was to destroy the existing public school system. Nine separate organizations joined together as the Committee to Educate Against Vouchers. They represented parents, teachers, school administrators, school employees, school

boards and community colleges. "The initiative," they charged, "isn't designed to improve the school system [but] to destroy it."

Joseph Alibrandi, long-time vigorous critic of the public school system and, as ExCel's co-chairman, the moving force behind the plan, denies any such intention. "The objective here is not to move kids out of public schools into private schools. The objective is to improve public schools." Yet, at another point during a lengthy interview, he said, "People can keep talking about reforms [of the public education system] and all the rest, but I've come to the conclusion the system is the problem. I've given up on it."

Mary Bergan, president of the California Federation of Teachers (CFT), labels the initiative "consumer fraud." Doing nothing to improve the ability of schools to correct faults in the system, she asserts, it gives money to families already sending their children to private school. Thus, she stresses, families unable to pay the difference between

Stanley Moss is freelance writer from Los Angeles.

$2600 and the "far higher tuition of the typical private school" will keep their children in the public system that ExCel criticizes as inadequate, and therefore they don't have the choice ExCel claims it wants for everybody.

William Anton, superintendent of the Los Angeles Unified School District (LAUSD), condemns the initiative as meaningless to most inner-city students who lack means of transportation to schools they might select. "What about youngsters with special needs?," he asks. Will private schools take those with physical handicaps or who don't speak English or don't meet certain levels of comprehension? Potentially, he said, white students are more likely to opt for the voucher and leave the system, emphasizing further the minority aspect of the district. "Obviously, the most immediate consequence," he notes, "will be loss of income when we already are deep in trouble."

Historically, vouchers to underwrite education of children can be traced back to 1776, when Adam Smith wrote about them in "Wealth of Nations" and suggested they be given to parents to enable them to buy the educational services they wanted for their children. Even Thomas Paine, a few years later, developed a plan to provide tax rebates to parents unable otherwise to afford education for their children. A century later, John Stuart Mill recommended government assistance for such families.

And almost 40 years ago, the noted conservative economist, Milton Friedman, in his book "Capitalism and Freedom," criticized the inefficiency of public schools, pointing to the absence of innovation as characteristic of monopolies. He wanted the government's role restricted, however, to financing independent schools that would be free to set their own admissions criteria, except they could not discriminate because of race, and would have to meet minimum health and safety standards. Students would be allowed to choose among these schools. None of these proposals got beyond the idea stage.

As chairman and CEO of a multi-million-dollar aerospace company, Alibrandi believes strongly in the corporate principle of "rewards for success ... penal[ties] for failure." He sees rewards and penalties as "key ingredients ... to produce excellence." The absence of these leave school administrators, prin-

cipals and teachers free to do less than their best, he feels. Fortified by lack of competition there is little incentive for them to satisfy the wishes and needs of parents and children. Heavy-handed bureaucracy and no real accountability for performance explain further, he says, why the system has failed.

Helen Bernstein, president of United Teachers of Los Angeles (UTLA), has a totally different perception of what ails public education. What appears to make her angriest are accusations that teachers simply don't care about the kids they teach, that they do less than their best because of the absence of rewards and penalties. "If a teacher is a bad teacher," she says, "there are plenty of rules to help that teacher out of the system. The person who dislikes a bad teacher most is another teacher."

As for the charge that it's the system's fault kids don't learn, she explodes pugnaciously. "Am I responsible because kids come to school unfed, underclothed, abused because of an alcoholic parent or because the family is so poor they have to pick crops in the middle of the semester? Am I responsible because someone threatened them on their way to school? Am I responsible for 60 percent of the kids on my class roll in September not being there in June?"

Bernstein yields to no one who criticizes the bureaucracy. "They want teachers to fit a mold and teach in a prescribed way." The cost of bureaucracy, she complains, deprives schools of much-needed supplies and books.

Bergan of CFT agrees. Teachers need more "real authority" in order to do their jobs right. "Too many dollars," she adds, "go to tracking other dollars to be sure money is well spent instead of those dollars going into classrooms."

A major contention of unfriendly critics of the existing school system is that, being a monopoly, it ignores the wishes of parents concerning the education they would like to see their children receive. Without competition that would spur correction of deficiencies, the system does little or nothing to improve teaching techniques, allow more creativity in the classroom and recognize the individuality of the children.

In a position paper this past December, the California Business Roundtable declared, "Market forces in some form are necessary ... However, public educa-

tion is a complex enterprise" so whatever is done "must be carefully crafted to avoid unintended consequences." The Roundtable paper continued that it favored choice as "one of several structural changes" but that widespread extension of school choice to private and religious schools should be considered only when the effects of public school choice and other structural changes now being proposed are proven inadequate."

Two important religious groups have grappled with the initiative and the promise of its munifience. Catholic parochial schools constitute a large number of private schools that might expect a substantial increase in enrollments if the initiative should become law, to say nothing of the welcome subsidy to their students enrolled as of October 1, 1991. Far smaller in number, schools for young Jews nonetheless occupy an indispensable role among the orthodox and are a priority concern among conservative Jews who want their children informed about their faith.

Dr. Jerome Porath, superintendent of the Department of Schools in the Los Angeles Archdiocese, is extremely cautious in stating the view of the hierarchy regarding Voucher/Choice. Understandably, the Archdiocese adopted a most politic stance: the Archdiocese, he says, has not taken a position and is unlikely to, but is leaving to parents and individuals within the parishes and school system the right to state their position. Recognizing the widespread feeling about the separation of church and state, it was deemed wiser not to announce official endorsement of Voucher/Choice since that would call unwelcome attention to the use of taxpayer money to subsidize parochial schools.

As for the Jewish community, the Jewish Federation Council of Greater Los Angeles adopted a strongly-worded resolution opposing the initiative and urged its officials and staff to "join in any coalition of like-minded organizations and institutions to inform and educate the public as to the harmful consequences of such proposals." One such organization, the California State PTA, had voted immediately after the launching of the initiative signature drive to reject the voucher-redeeming plan as designed to steal dollars from underfunded public schools to ease the burden of private school fees on the "wealthy."

Ralph Flynn, executive director of the California Teachers Association

(CTA), described the cost to public education of the Voucher/Choice plan as "humungous," spelling out some details. Every student who withdraws from one public school to go to another takes along a $2600 voucher to give to the school of his/her choice. According to Flynn, the school from which he/she has withdrawn loses not only the $2600 but the entire $5200 it was receiving for that student. If any important number of students leave a particular school and are not replaced to any extent, the school, probably already lacking sufficient funds, would be defunct and unable in any practical sense to serve its remaining students.

Virgil Roberts, president of a prominent record company and an Alibrandi colleague in another organization seeking to improve public education, said Alibrandi did have an interest in helping low-income minority kids get a better education. "But," he added, "this initiative doesn't do it. It comes across basically as a way for private schools to gain access to public funds."

The Los Angeles Educational Alliance for Restructuring Now (known as Learn), whose president and CEO is former Democratic Assemblyman Mike Roos, has been painstaking in its study of the problems confronting public education. Its advisory board is composed of outstanding business executives, educators and civic organizations. Despite the fact that Alibrandi, of ExCel, is a member of the board as a representative of the California Business Roundtable, Learn was forthright in describing the Voucher/Choice initiative as "ill-conceived" and 'promis[ing] a 'magic bullet' solution-educational vouchers." Learn favors choice within the school system but adds, "By itself, choice cannot assure quality education for all students."

The initiative contains various other controversial features. The vouchers are not to be taxable as income; schools with as few as 25 students are eligible to accept vouchers; teachers need not be credentialed; no new regulations can be placed on private schools, voucher-redeeming or not, unless confirmed by a three-fourths vote of the Legislature or two-thirds vote of the local government body plus a majority vote by people within the local jurisdiction.

But, saving the most controversial condition after the voucher itself for last, the initiative requires that, "Within one year ... the Legislature shall establish an expeditous process by which public schools may become independent scholarship-redeeming schools" and operate as private schools. This doesn't exactly square with initiative proponents' claim that they don't want the public education system broken up.

Apparently timed in tandem with distribution of initiative petitions, GOP state Senator Bill Leonard of Upland sent the Senate Education Committee his bill, SCA 30, to amend the state Constitution. The wording of the bill is identical with that of the initiative. Leonard says the initiative proposal is "the fail-safe" device if the Legislature fails to do its job," meaning passage of his bill to amend the state Constitution. He doesn't hold out much hope for the bill's success, however.

"The bureaucrats who control education have their people on the [education] committees and probably will kill" it, he predicts. Leonard says he is "not out to subsidize private schools or destroy public schools. I want to break the back of bureaucracy that ... is stifling public education." He adds that, although he is "convinced" the voucher/choice idea is the only way to achieve needed changes in public education, "if there's a better way, yes, I'd consider it. ... My mind is not closed."

In February, the chairman of the Senate Education Committee, Democrat Gary Hart of Santa Barbara, and his Assembly counterpart, Democrat Delaine Eastin of Fremont, announced separately their introduction of separate bills calling for the establishment of "charter schools." Asked if they had worked together in framing their bills, Hart said neither knew what the other was doing but when he heard about the Eastin bill, he contacted her and they agreed to work together. There are some differences in the bills but, according to Martha Martinez, an Eastin aide, they should not be insurmountable.

Because of stepped-up activity regarding public education, and particularly the emergence of school vouchers into the spotlight, the stage may be set for legislation to experiment with the charter school concepts. In brief, the bills provide for charter schools to be like a school district, receiving state funding but not subject to laws generally governing school districts, being free to devise programs of a wide variety, to function more flexibly and to handle their own budget. They would be public schools with a revocable charter for up to five years and renewable for another five years. The number of such schools would be held to 100 in any school year. These schools are intended to "encourage the use of different and innovative teaching methods that improve pupil learning" and to give teachers greater responsibility for creating programs at the school site, thereby offering expanded educational opportunities within the public school system.

After the proposals on charter schools were announced, Leonard was reminded of his comment that his "mind is not closed" and he would consider other ways than vouchers to improve public education. In response he said, "My goal is to empower parents to have quality choices about the education of their children. Any program that does that I'm going to look at and be open-minded about — absolutely."

It is increasingly clear that California's public school system is on the cusp of important change. 🏛